Walking Perthshire

Clan Walk Guides

Walking Perthshire

Walking Scotland Series
Volume 4

Mary Welsh

Maps and Illustrations by
Christine Isherwood

First published Westmorland Gazette, 1992 as *Walks in Perthshire*
Revised edition published by Clan Books, 2000
Reprinted 2003
This new re-titled edition published by Clan Books, 2009

ISBN 978 1873597 31 6
Text © Mary Welsh 2009
Maps and Illustrations
© Christine Isherwood 2009

Clan Books
Clandon House
The Cross, Doune
Perthshire
FK16 6BE

Printed and bound in Great Britain by
Bell & Bain Ltd., Glasgow

Publisher's Note

The original *Walks in Perthshire* was published in 1992. In 2000, a new edition published by Clan Books celebrated the title's re-birth in its "home county" by introducing a number of exciting new expeditions, replacing a few of the more bland ones in the original.

Now adopting the new series format title *Walking Perthshire*, we are introducing several new walks which we hope our active readers will find stimulating. Also included are walks around Killin, using material first published in *Walking the Trossachs, Loch Lomondside and the Campsie Fells* (2005), having decided that these really belong within the entity of Perthshire.

The Author's Golden Rules
for Good, Safe Walking

- Wear suitable clothes and take adequate waterproofs.
- Walk in strong footwear; walking boots are advisable.
- Carry the relevant map and a compass and know how to use them.
- Carry a whistle; remember six long blasts repeated at one minute intervals is the distress signal.
- Do not walk alone, and tell someone where you are going.
- If mist descends, return.
- Keep all dogs under strict control. Observe all "No Dogs" notices – they are there for very good reasons.

In all volumes of the WALKING SCOTLAND series, the authors make every effort to ensure accuracy, but changes can occur after publication. Reports of such changes are welcomed by the publisher. Neither the publisher nor the authors can accept responsibility for errors, omissions or any loss or injury.

Contents

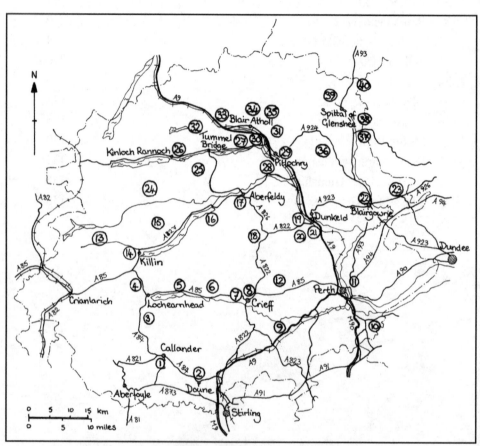

N

<!-- Map labels -->
A 93

A 9

40

39

32 33 34 35
    Blair Atholl

Tummel 27 30 31
Bridge   Spittal of
                  Glenshee 38

Kinloch Rannoch 26   A 924   37

                  25   29 36
                      28 Pitlochry

                  Aberfeldy
24   17   A 923   23
                                              22
        15   16   A 926 A 94
                        A 827   18   A 923
13   19 Dunkeld Blairgowrie

                        18 A 822
14 Killin   20 21
                                      A 9   A 923   Dundee
                                          A 93 A 94
A 85   A 923
        4   5 A 85 6   12 A 85
    Lochearnhead 7 8   Perth
A 82 Crianlarich   Crieff   11
                  3   9   10

                  Callander
A 821   1   A 84
A 84   2   A 9   A 823
    Aberfoyle A 873 Doune   A 91   A 91
                        A 91
0 5 10 15 km A 81   Stirling
0   5   10 miles   A 9

County of Perthshire

1

Callander

Park in the riverside car park on the south side of Callander's Main Street, grid ref 626079.

Callander: The small town, busy with visitors during the summer and week-ends, is known as the Gateway to the Trossachs and became familiar to TV viewers a few years ago as "Tannochbrae", the setting for "Dr Finlay's Casebook".

The walk description here is diverted from the original version (*Walks in Perthshire, 2000 Edition*) because of the destruction of the Bridge of Brackland above the Bracklinn Falls, during flash floods in 2004.

Bracklinn Falls, Callander

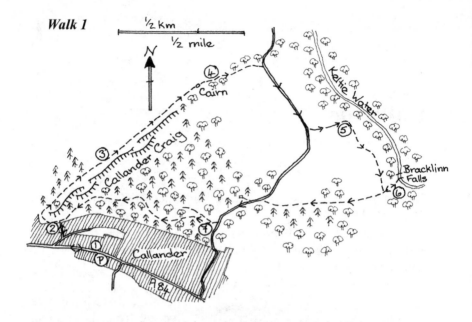

Walk 1

½ km

½ mile

N

Cairn

④

Callander Craig

③

Keltie Water

⑤

Bracklinn Falls

⑥

②

⑦

①

P

Callander

A84

1 From the car park, return to the street. Turn left and, remaining on the same side of the road, walk on in the direction of The Trossachs and Crianlarich. Ignore the cycleway going off left, and here cross the road to go down a turning by the Tulipan Lodge Hotel. Follow a signpost, sometimes obscured by foliage in the summer, directing you left for 'The Crags and Wood Walks'.

2 Immediately beyond a Forestry Commission (FC) sign, turn left for the Crags walking the footpath which starts uphill at a steady gradient. This level-surfaced and well-drained track could easily be mistaken for a forestry vehicle road, if it were a metre or so wider. It replaces the eroded old route of ascent marked on all the maps as hugging the course of an old wall. Soon the walkway merges into the traditional path and the views start to open out, with, to the west and north, Ben Ledi close and majestic. Then through widening gaps in the trees you have fine southern views over Callander and towards the upper Forth Valley and the Campsie Fells.

3 Then the path continues with all the characteristics of a mountain ridge-walk, entailing minor scrambles up and down rocky steps. The high point is marked by a substantial cairn, erected in 1897, and marking Queen Victoria's Diamond Jubilee. The panoramic view fills in all the gaps from the earlier glimpses; Loch Venachar and the Trossachs to

the west, Stuc a' Chroin and Ben Vorlich to the north. To the east, on a clear day, there is a fine prospect over Stirling with, spread out in a line, the castle, Wallace Monument and the little hill of Dumyat.

4 Continue along the ridge, which descends gradually at first and then more steeply. Finally, the path drops through dense woodland to a single-track road. Turn right down the unfenced way for about 500yds/0.5km. Pass a water installation on the right with a ruinous concrete hut, and look ahead over to the left for the posts of a broken wire fence crossing the tussocky open ground. Leave the road at any suitable point and follow the line of the fence down to where it meets a wall at a corner, just beyond a clump of trees. There is no real path here, and the going is heavy but the wall is soon reached.

5 Cross the wall at an easy place at the corner and follow it right, with first bracken and then conifers on the left. Pass a broken metal gate and continue in open ground beside the wall until you pick up an indistinct path which goes, left, down the slope past the corner of the conifer plantation. Soon the path bears right, leaving the trees behind and dropping down the slope through a gap between bracken and gorse to reach the main path leading to Bracklinn Falls. Turn left down the steps to view the impressive waterfall.

6 When you are ready to drag yourself away from this exciting site, go back up the steps and continue along the main path to reach the road by a car park. You rejoin the road walked earlier; follow it down to the left, passing a turn to a reservoir, then turning right into the woods at a FC sign.

7 Soon fork left off the main forestry track with its wide vehicle access barrier, and where the way divides, take the straight-ahead route. Climb steps to cross a footbridge, descending by more steps on the other side and go on. Ignore the track on the right. This is signed by a red-striped marker post and denotes the start of 400 steps to the top of the Crags. The woodland way descends steadily until you arrive at the point where you started to climb at the outset of the walk. Retrace your outward route to return to the car park.

Meadow Cranesbill

Type of walk: Good paths take you through woodland and on to the Crags above Callander, from where you can enjoy stunning views; then down and over rough ground to reach the spectacular Bracklinn Falls. Sadly, the footbridge giving the best view was swept away in the 2004 floods.

Total distance:	4 miles/6.5km
Time:	2½ hours
Map:	OS Landranger 57/Explorer 368

Red Kite
One of the sites chosen for the re-introduction of these magnificent birds is at Argaty, near Doune. They can often be seen searching for carrion on the braes above Doune and Callander.

2

Doune Castle, the Ponds and Commonty Walk

To reach the castle car park, grid ref 728012, enter the approach road from the direction of the town centre, rather than from the Dunblane road, because of the acute angle of turn. Go on past the church on the left, fork right after a narrow downward slope and then on along a road signposted to the castle. A visit to this fine castle is well worth while.

Doune and its Castle. Doune is one of Scotland's earliest burghs, with a charter granted by King James 1611. Its medieval castle is one of the best preserved in Scotland, which is not only steeped in history but has been much favoured by film-makers because of its well preserved walls and battlements, and its commanding site on a rocky outcrop above two rivers.

Doune Castle

Salmon spend their adult life in the sea. Then, at maturity they return to the quiet inland streams where they were spawned. To reach them they battle against rushing torrents to leap headlong up swift waterfalls or fish-ladders provided to help them scale impeding weirs. In the clear well-oxygenated water and gravelly beds of the streams the females lay their eggs and the males fertilise them, and soon afterwards the adults die. The eggs, sometimes 10,000 alone from one female, thrive in shallow fast-running water. In about two months or more the young burst forth from the eggs. They carry a huge yolk-sac, which nourishes them in the early weeks. Some months later they venture forth as free-swimming fry, and in about a year they set off downstream. After several years at sea they return, often to the same river where they hatched, probably drawn by memory of the smell.

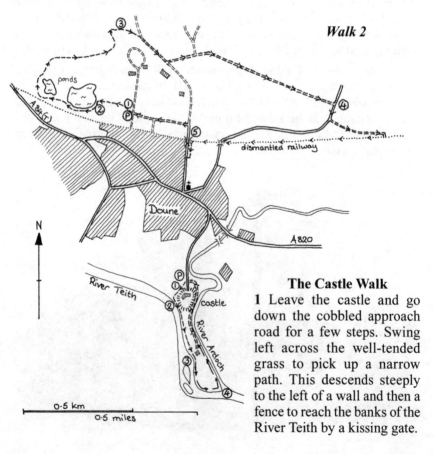

Walk 2

The Castle Walk

1 Leave the castle and go down the cobbled approach road for a few steps. Swing left across the well-tended grass to pick up a narrow path. This descends steeply to the left of a wall and then a fence to reach the banks of the River Teith by a kissing gate.

2 Do not go through the gate, but turn left along a narrow but well used path which undulates along the high bank of the fast-flowing Teith. Pass a fine deep pool, which briefly halts the speeding surface waters and into which local anglers still occasionally lure wild salmon.

3 On reaching an open area of more level ground continue close to the river. At this point, especially if you are an early morning visitor, you may hear the lions roaring for their breakfast in the woods of the Blair Drummond Safari Park.

4 At the confluence of the River Ardoch with the Teith, go round and back along the bank of the tributary river. Follow the track past the castle on its rocky pedestal up to your left, and return to your car.

The Ponds and Commonty (Common land) Walk

Park in the car park on the north side of Doune, grid ref 726018. To reach this, leave the A820, on its north side, with the parish church on your right. Follow the signposted 'Nature Trail' to go over the bridge and turn left for 'Doune Ponds,' which takes you to the parking area.

1 Pick up a leaflet from a dispenser by the kissing gate. Beyond, go straight ahead, ignoring tracks to either side until you see the central pond ahead of you at a picnic area with a wooden platform by the pond. Here various species of duck, coot, moorhen and, occasionally swans, congregate, hoping to be fed.

2 With your back to the pond follow the track right which takes you round beside the pond. Pass a birdwatchers' hide and, bearing right past marker post 2, take the sometimes muddy pond-side track. A second hide is seen by the waymark post 3. The path now winds up into a conifer plantation. Ignore steps going down to the left and walk through trees to cross a wooden platform at marker post 4. Keep to

Coot and Waterlilies

the lower level route, which passes marker post 5 and descends into a grove of downy birch, where wild orchids may be found among the buttercups and wild strawberries. In the later months this is also a good spot for finding various fungi. Pass waymark 6, and when the path rises to a junction at marker 7, go ahead along a gravelled section until reaching open ground.

3 Here marker 8 directs you to the left through silver birch. Take the steps up the steep brae. At the top, press on ahead to join a rutted estate road going downhill for about 100m, then follow the signpost for the Commonty Walk uphill to the left. This soon becomes a terrace walk along a tree-lined track. To the right, fine views open up across Doune to the Carse of Stirling and the Campsie Fells, with Ben Lomond to the far right. Looking at this peaceful prospect, it is hard to believe that the vast Glasgow and Clydebank conurbation lies less than ten miles beyond the skyline.

4 On reaching a road, turn right and then follow the signposted "Doune Trail" left along a track between conifer plantations. Look north where trees have been felled; you may see red kites. Before the track enters a field, take a few steps down to the right, taking you to a track recently tarmacked to "upgrade" it as a cycle track. Ben Ledi, Callander's presiding mountain, can be seen just off to the right as you emerge from a cutting: the cutting evidence that you are following the bed of the former Callander and Oban Railway.

5 When the tarmac ends, continue for a short distance along the old railway track, then turn left before reaching a bridge, past a fenced and surfaced sports compound and take a gate on the right to join a road, over the bridge. This is the road you drove down earlier and by turning left and walking a short distance you regain the car park.

Practicals

Type of walk: Two delightful walks close to the charming town of Doune.

Castle Walk

Total distance:	¾ miles/1.3km
Time:	½ hour

Ponds and Commonty Walk

Total distance:	3½ miles/5.5km
Time:	1½ hours
Maps:	OS Landranger 57/Explorer 366

3

Linear walk from Edinample by Loch Earn via Stuc a'Chroin and Beinn Each to Ardchullarie More on Loch Lubnaig

This is a full-day linear walk, best attempted on a reliably clear day by a party of walkers with two cars. Park one car in the big layby found on the east side (right going north) of the A84, 4 miles/6.5km south of Strathyre, grid ref 585137 close to the farmhouse, Ardchullarie More.

Park the second car at Edinample, grid ref 602225 This is reached by driving 8 miles/13km north towards Lochearnhead, and then as you descend towards the loch and the village, look for the single track road, off right, signposted South Loch Earn Road. Follow this road to the hamlet of Edinample to park on the verge, on the right, before the bridge, ensuring that you do not obstruct the access to the track up the glen.

Stuc a' Chroin and Beinn Each from Glen Ogle

Edinample Falls. The Burn of Ample descends steeply, in three cascades, 60ft/18m in total, in the direction of Loch Earn. The cascades are a fine sight at any time, but are really dramatic after a prolonged wet spell.

Stuc a'Chroin: the peak of harm or danger (not really if you take care). On a clear day the view from this Munro (see Walk 40) is stunning. Stirling and the Forth estuary lie far away to the south-east, with the rounded Ochils above. The prospect eastwards is dramatically interrupted by the rocky top of Ben Vorlich close by. Then the eye can sweep around in an unbroken arc from Ben Lawers in the north, by Ben More and the high tops surrounding Crianlarich to Ben Lomond, behind and just to the right of Ben Ledi.

Corbetts. Between the two world wars, John Rooke Corbett was a keen member of the Scottish Mountaineering Club. He listed all those mountains that ranged in height between 762m and 915m (2500ft and 3000ft) and that had a drop of 153m/500ft around their summits. There are 221 mountains in his list including Beinn Each which is climbed on this walk.

1 Stride up the Glen Ample track, with the falls of Edinample on your left. Almost immediately the track divides and you take the left fork to continue steadily upward, close to the wooded banks of the Burn of Ample. The main track swings left over a bridge to the house of Glenample. Here go on along the narrower path which continues on the left (west) bank, with a deer fence on the right. Cross the burn by a wooden footbridge and take the red arrowed route up through the trees opposite. This gives access to the track coming out of the farm on the left, which you follow as it climbs through young but rapidly growing conifers.

2 Cross a stile and emerge from the trees on to the open hillside. From the continuing track there are fine and steadily expanding views of the high hills around, with the massive bulk of Ben Vorlich ahead and above. Then the track suddenly peters out. Here continue ahead, following the main burn and then making for the lowest point of the skyline to reach the Coire Fuadarach and on to the saddle – Bealach an Dubh Choirein. Look and listen for red grouse as you go.

Walk 3

3 Join the climbers' track from the saddle, which steeply ascends the imposing rock face of Stuc a'Chroin. The experienced scrambler may be tempted to seek a route directly up the crag, but the more cautious should turn right, on reaching the rocks, to take the steep but safe narrow path which starts upwards from about 50m/150ft to the north-west. This leads to the summit plateau of the great buttress. Follow the fence posts south to arrive at the summit cairn, 975m/3189ft.

4 Several ridges radiate from the summit plateau. It is important, especially if clouds come down unexpectedly, to ensure that you leave the top walking due west, with fence posts and an intermittent pyouath marking the route along the winding ridge. This turns south and then west again, dropping to the Bealach Glas. Beyond this, the ridge establishes a southerly course as it rises to a knobbly but unnamed subsidiary summit.

5 Descend to the Bealach-nan-Cabar and then climb again to the summit of Beinn Each, 813m/2604ft, not a Munro but a Corbett.

6 From the summit take a faint path, descending the nose westwards, beside the line of fence posts. This turns down from the summit and

leads to craggy outcrops. To avoid these bear left (south) down a steep slope to pick up the headwaters of the delightful Eas an Eoin, and follow this as it tumbles steeply down to the valley. Keep to the right (north) bank, where there are traces of a path.

7 On reaching the track coming over the pass from Glen Ample, turn left and make for the plantation below. Beyond the forest fence the walkers' path down to Ardchullarie More diverges right from the forest track, keeping close to the burn on the right. Continue on to join the road. Turn right for a few steps to reach the layby.

Red grouse in heather

NB The walk could be attempted by leaving a car at the Ardchullarie More layby, timing arrival there to enable you to take one of the occasional Stirling to Killin service buses, or a post bus which starts from Callander. Get off the bus at South Loch Earn Road junction and walk just less than a mile to Glen Ample track. Check bus times at Rob Roy Tourist Centre, Callander (Tel. 01877 330342).

NB For two car walk, don't forget to take all your equipment and supplies for a long day for the whole party.

Practicals

Type of walk: A challenging, rewarding walk. It starts with a pleasant riverside stroll up a wooded glen, it continues by ascending a wild corrie and culminates in a rocky scramble to the peak of a Munro. Then it goes on along a wide and winding ridge to the summit of a Corbett, followed by a steep descent to valley level. Do NOT attempt in the mist.

Total distance:	10 miles/16km
Time:	8 hours
Maps:	Harveys Superwalker Ben Ledi (1-25,000)
	OS Landrangers 51 and 57
	OS Explorer 365 and 368

4

Lochearnhead to Killin:
The Railway Trail

The spectacular former railway trackbed over Glenoglehead forms part of the route of each of the four options described in this chapter:

4a – Linear walk from Lochearnhead to Killin;

4b – Linear walk from Killin to Lochearnhead;

4c – Circular walk from Lochearnhead;

4d – Circular walk from Killin.

Parking for walks starting from Lochearnhead is at the public car park a short distance east along the A85 from its junction with the A84, grid ref 593208. Killin has several car parks, the most convenient being at grid ref 573326, about 72yds/70m along from the River Dochart bridge.

Viaduct, Glen Ogle

Callander and Oban Railway. Opened in 1880, the railway was "grouped" into the LMSR in 1923. It had been absorbed by British Railways when, in 1965, the line was blocked by great boulders, torn from the crags above Glen Ogle by frost and heavy rain,

creating a massive landslide. This
justified the immediate closure
of a line already threatened by
Dr Beeching's axe. The section
running up Glen Ogle now
forms part of National
Cycle Route 7, and
is surfaced for
the benefit of
cyclists.

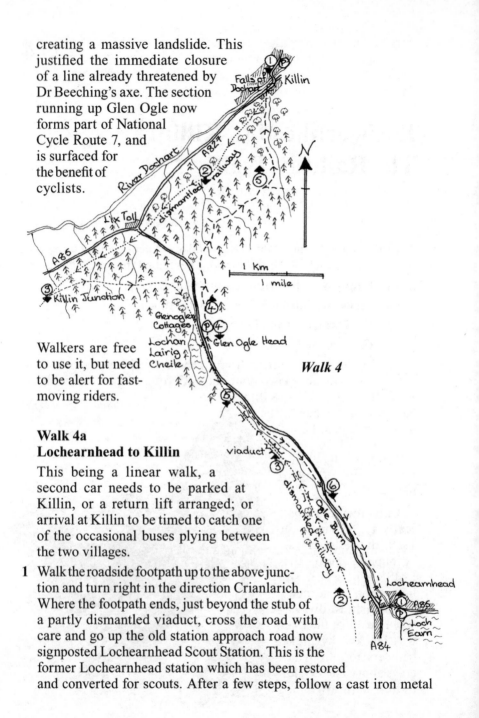

Walkers are free
to use it, but need
to be alert for fast-
moving riders.

Walk 4

Walk 4a
Lochearnhead to Killin

This being a linear walk, a
second car needs to be parked at
Killin, or a return lift arranged; or
arrival at Killin to be timed to catch one
of the occasional buses plying between
the two villages.

1 Walk the roadside footpath up to the above junction and turn right in the direction Crianlarich.
Where the footpath ends, just beyond the stub of
a partly dismantled viaduct, cross the road with
care and go up the old station approach road now
signposted Lochearnhead Scout Station. This is the
former Lochearnhead station which has been restored
and converted for scouts. After a few steps, follow a cast iron metal

signpost for the Glen Ogle Trail, which directs you steeply up through the trees to a gate through a high fence. This gives you access to the former railway trackbed perched on the hillside 100yds/91m up. As you climb look back for a good view over the village to Loch Earn and the hills beyond. From this point and throughout, the Glen Ogle Trail is clearly waymarked by yellow arrows on short stakes.

2 Turn right along the track, now used as a cycle track as well as a walkers' route, and stride out along the steadily-rising evenly graded terrace through the trees that now surround it. Overhead you might spot a pair of buzzards circling on the rmals. The track continues to climb, coming to a section where the ravages of past severe winters are awesomely visible – a landslide in 1965 brought about the closure of the line.

3 Follow the track across the curving stone viaduct and, near the top of the glen, keep with the cycle track as it veers to the right and reaches the A85 road. Cross with great care and continue parallel with the road to reach the car park at the pass summit, where there is often a welcome mobile snack bar parked. Go on a little further to enjoy the panoramic view of the Munros beyond Killin from Meall nan Tarmachan to the Ben Lawers massif.

4 Go on under the overhead barrier and continue along the track. Pass through a deer gate and turn left to walk the tarmacked cycle track, downhill, passing through yellow bollards. Eventually the tarmac ends and a pleasing track, with grass down the middle, continues. Ahead is another magnificent view of the Ben Lawers range. Carry on to reach a T-junction of tracks, where you turn right. The route now makes a wide semi-circle, rising steadily, through mixed woodland where you might spot roe deer, woodpecker, jay, hen harrier and, at the right time of the year, a host of dragonflies and common blue butterflies. Soon the track levels and on the banks you might see stag's horn clubmoss.

Buzzard

5 At the T-junction, take the left branch and begin to descend steadily, with Killin soon coming into view. Pass through a deer gate and walk beside the A827, eastwards. Reaching the River Dochart Bridge, try to stop as you cross, while keeping clear of

passing motor traffic, to look upstream and see the magnificent Falls of Dochart. Turn right at the far side and find your car park.

Walk 4b Killin to Lochearnhead

The starting and finishing points of this walk are the reverse of those in the previous walk, but it follows a different route. Similar transport parameters for a linear walk apply, of course. A second car parked at Lochearnhead, a lift back to Killin, or an assignment with one of the occasional Lochearnhead-Killin buses are the options (unless you want to walk all the way back).

1 Turn left out of the car park to cross the bridge over the River Dochart, admiring the rapids of the Dochart Falls to the right whilst watching out for road traffic on this narrow crossing. Continue beside the A827 road to the right and on reaching the war memorial take a gravel track opposite on the left, just before two bungalows. Follow the cycle sign through a pedestrian gate beside a locked deer gate, then turn off right to walk the track of the short-lived Killin branch of the Callander and Oban railway. The track passes through deciduous woodland. Look right towards a pond beyond the trees where roe deer are sometimes seen grazing. When the deer fencing ends the track continues between plantations where long-tailed tits may be seen.

2 On reaching a crossroads of tracks, go ahead on a narrower raised track, still the old railway line. Go through a deer fence and beyond the track opens out as you head for the A85. Cross with great care, checking that both ways are clear, and carry on up the sloping track through clear fell to rejoin the railway line. Stroll on with a sudden brief view of Glen Dochart to the west. Ignore a track coming in on your left and carry on a short distance to arrive at the old platform of Killin Junction.

3 After a pause in this quiet area, walk back to the Y-junction and take the right branch which follows the track of the main Oban-Callander line. It climbs almost imperceptibly, to the summit at Glenoglehead. As you reach Glenogle cottages on the left, look for a narrow path just before the buildings and go through the hedge to the main A85 road. Cross with care and walk right for a short distance to enter the car park at the pass summit, where you may find the mobile snack bar. Walk a short way left to enjoy the wide mountain panorama culminating in the 3984ft/1214m Ben Lawers.

4 Walk back through the car park and take the cycle track running south parallel with the road, and where it turns to cross the road, continue

Falls of Dochart

to follow it, under a bridge in a cutting. Soon after, look for a footpath waymark up the embankment on the left.

5 Cross the ladder stile over the fence, and follow the grassy and sometimes boggy path down the glen marked with yellow arrows. The waters forming the Ogle Burn are crossed by stepping stones and the route follows down the left bank. You may pass the waterfalls seen from the road, which are very impressive, especially after prolonged rain.

6 The path winds through trees and reaches a stile on to the A85. Go straight across to follow a narrow path keeping well above the road and farm buildings. Two stiles and a tributary burn are crossed in quick succession and the path continues, clearly waymarked until a footbridge over the Ogle Burn leads back up to the road, under the old railway viaduct. Follow the roadside footpath and turn left down the A85 for about ¼ mile/0.5km to reach the car park.

Walk 4c Circular Walk from Lochearnhead to Glenoglehead

Outward: Follow instructions in paragraph 1-3 of walk 4a above. These take you as far as the Glenoglehead viewpoint, the objective of the walk.

Return: Follow instructions in paragraphs 4–6 of Walk 4b, returning to Lochearnhead by the route down the glen.

Walk 4d Circular Walk from Killin to Glenoglehead

Outward: Follow instructions in paragraphs 1–3 of Walk 4b above. These take you to the Glenoglehead viewpoint, returning by a different route.

Return: Follow instructions in paragraphs 4–5 of Walk 4a, returning to Killin mainly down open hillside with great views.

A Challenge to strong, ambitious walkers

Given time and energy the full walk can be done in both directions in a day. It is just over 17 miles/27km and if route 4a is used northwards and 4b southwards (starting from either end), a very satisfactory "figure of 8" walk is completed. Some time and distance can be saved on the southbound walk, if you don't want to visit the Glenoglehead car park/viewpoint twice, by keeping straight on down the railway track when you reach Glenogle Cottages, picking up 4b again at the footpath waymark beyond the overbridge (paragraph 5).

Long-tailed tit

Practicals

Type of Walk: All four options use the easy-going old railway track bed and visit the fine viewpoint at the head of Glen Ogle. The paths followed for descent are also clear and mainly gently graded.

Total distances:	**4a** – 7½ mile/12km
	4b – 10 miles/16km
	4c – 10 miles/16km
	4d – 9 miles/14km
Time:	3½, 4, 4, 3¾ hours respectively
Maps:	OS Landranger 51/Explorers 365 and 378

5

Goat's Path and Glentarken Wood, St Fillans

Park in a large lay-by at the east end of Loch Earn, west of St Fillans and beyond the Four Seasons Hotel, grid ref 689246.

Neish Island The island lies just off shore. This is a crannog or man-made island dating back to prehistoric lake-dwellers. In 1612 a particularly bloody massacre occurred when the island was occupied by the McNeishes. They allowed only their own boats on Loch Earn. Their traditional enemies were the McNabs from Killin. One night the McNeishes waylaid a McNab servant carrying provisons. A few days later the McNabs, under the cover of darkness, carried out a surprise attack on the island, and massacred all except one small boy. The severed head of the McNeish chieftain was carried back to Killin.

Viaduct,
Glentarken Path

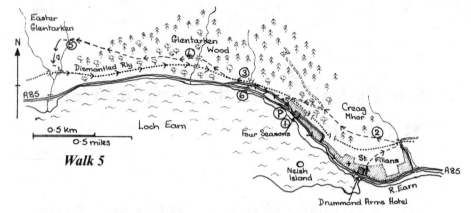

Walk 5

1 Take the roadside path past the Four Seasons and go on to pass the Drummond Arms Hotel. As you go look for Neish Island, just off shore. Immediately beyond the hotel, turn left into Shoemaker's Lane and walk to the end. Go through the gateway and follow a narrow path bearing slightly right to pass through a small oak wood. Continue on the path through pasture to a gate. Turn left between the buttresses of the old railway embankment. Ignore the turning to the A-frame houses. Beyond, go left through a farm gate signposted Goat's Walk. The track ahead soon becomes a narrow path. Go off left through the bracken, with the path climbing gently, keeping parallel with the disused railway.

2 Beyond the next gate you now reach the Goat's Path; it is named after the wild goats that once grazed the pastures. Stroll the ascending path, enjoying the splendid views ahead of Loch Earn and its attend-ant mountains. From the fir plantation, to the right, come the quiet whisperings of goldcrest and coal tit. Go on along the path over the scree of Creag Mhor and on through, in mid summer, heather, golden rod, harebells, bedstraw and foxgloves. Ahead the loch stretches away, breathtakingly lovely. Head into a plantation of firs and then, beyond, an open area with two seats well placed for enjoying the view. Continue through more firs to reach a track. Turn left and walk downhill. Cross the railway bridge and drop down to the track coming up from the lochside to the left. Bear right by a wooden garage and follow this track through deciduous woodland, with more views of Loch Earn. Cross a small burn and walk beside a two arched railway bridge. Walk on for 100 yds/91m for access, on the right, to the old railway track. The wide stony way is shaded by young birch and you have delightful brief glimpses of the loch.

3 Cross a small viaduct, with a good view of a waterfall to your right and then a bridge with metal rails. Just beyond, on the right, take the narrow path that leads on, steadily upwards, through bracken and into Glentarken Wood. The way continues through alders and then deep into mixed woodland and comes to a burn. Cross by a stout wooden footbridge built by the Royal Engineer reservists in 1996.

4 Stride into oak woodland. This was once coppiced. Look for the many stems or stumps at the base of each tree. Head on along the path as it moves into firs before reaching a gate. Go ahead along a rather soft, muddy track where you will have to pick your own way. Emerge from the trees through a gateway, with the remains of a former iron gate. All about lies the evidence of the deserted settlement of Easter Glentarken where twelve families lived before the Highland Clearances. Follow the indistinct track as it wends through bracken. Progress over another very wet path, helped on your way by grand views of Loch Earn.

5 Pass through a gate in the fence and cross a small burn. Beyond, drop down over the steepish slopes on the left. Very soon a narrow path becomes evident. Follow it downhill and, where it begins to swing left, step over a stream, the same one crossed at the top of the slope. Climb the right hand fence onto the railway track and turn left to pass beneath a bridge. Beyond, a narrow path weaving through a jungle of nettles soon becomes a delightful track. To the left deciduous trees slope upwards to the left and birch slope down towards the loch.

6 Cross the five-arched viaduct over the white topped waterfall and walk on, making a right turn to leave the track. Continue ahead to join the reinforced track that leads down to the road (A85) by the loch. A few steps to the right takes you back to the layby.

Coal Tit

Practicals

A pleasing generally easy walk with exciting views of a lovely loch and its surrounding hills and mountains.

Total distance:	5 miles/8km
Time:	3–4 hours
Maps:	OS Landranger 51/Explorer 368

6

Glen Lednock, Comrie

Park in the Primary School car park at Comrie, grid ref 773221.

Comrie. Comrie is a Gaelic name, meaning 'confluence of streams'. The waters of Ruchill, the Earn and the Lednock come together at the village. The Romans occupied the area until the third century A.D. Comrie suffered from the plague and from a small pox epidemic. Its people always considered itself a Highland village and in the past spoke Gaelic. They sympathised with the Jacobites but, unlike Crieff, the town was not burnt to the ground. It is famous as Britain's earthquake centre. It suffers mild earthquakes because it lies on the Highland Boundary Fault. Here two geological areas meet and even after many millions of years the two have not knitted together.

Shaky bridge

Deil's Caldron means Devil's Kettle – an apt name for this hollow in the ravine where the Lednock has cut a narrow passage. Stones and sand carried by the burn swirl round and round, cutting a large kettle-shaped pothole. In time the river breaks through and plunges as a fall into another basin. Legend has it that it was the favourite haunt of a water elf who enticed victims down the huge pothole.

Melville Monument was built on the top of Dun More in 1811. It commemorates Lord Melville, Henry Dundas, who was chief minister in Scotland under William Pitt the younger. The obelisk is 72ft/22m high and, when it was struck by lightning in 1894, the steeplejack who repaired it, reported that from its summit he could see Castle Rock in Edinburgh.

1 From the car park go right along the main street until it turns sharply left. At this corner carry straight on up Monument Street which leads up Glen Lednock. In 200yds/183m turn right to follow a path that skirts a field. Soon the path curves round into the wooded glen. Continue on to take another path to the right. This is railed and leads down to a fenced viewing area above the Wee Caldron, a set of rapids, in a noisy hollow, which is shaded with oak, rowan and beech. Over the swirling water a tiny wren flits back and forth.

2 Return to the main way via a few steps and a narrow path and walk on. The path runs close to the road but does not join it. It continues past a hut to a railed wooden walkway and a series of wooden steps, which lead down to a platform over Deil's Caldron, the spectacular waterfall. Leave by another railed way which takes you up to the road. Turn right and after 55yds/50m take the signposted gated path on the left, where a narrow, partly-stepped way leads upwards through the conifers

29

of Dun More. Towards the top, the path zigzags through heather to the railed obelisk. The view is breathtaking. Look north to see Ben Chronzie. To its left stands the huge dam of Loch Lednock, specially reinforced to withstand earthquakes. Bright patches of blue to the west are the waters of Loch Earn.

3   On leaving the monument, go down beyond the first zig-zag in the trees to reach a point where an alternative track diverges from the ascent route. Continue on this, descending steadily through the forest in a northerly direction. Soon the track leaves the plantation by a gate, with a stile, and moves on to the open hillside. There is now a grand view across the Lednock valley and of the hills on either side. Follow the track until you can turn off to the right, descending fairly steeply, at first, to the road below.

4   A few steps along to the right will bring you to a waymark indicating a sharp turn back to the left for Laggan Wood, your return route to Comrie. This track leads downhill towards a footbridge known locally as 'Shaky Bridge', since the original structure was distinctly wobbly. Its modern replacement appears to be completely rigid, but retains the interesting feature of being attached to the crook of a double-trunked sycamore half way along.

5   Cross the bridge, turn right along the narrow path beside the alder-lined burn. Climb the stile and then the steps beyond that lead up a slope covered with bracken. Follow the waymarked wide grassy path. Look right to see Lord Melville's monument towering above the firs and birch that find a foothold on the almost sheer sides of the crag. A waymark directs you slightly left, away from the lovely river, then climbs steadily to a kissing gate into Laggan Wood. Go on through oak woodland to follow the path as it drops downhill with firs to the left and oak to the right. Look for the waymark

Roe deer

where the firs crowd in on both sides. This directs you to a path on the right of the forest walk but still continuing ahead. Very soon you pass into more oak woodland, where you might see roe deer, and the path leads to a stepped and railed steep descent.

6 Before you descend head on to a heather-clad clearing with a seat. From here you have a fine view over Comrie, and its white church with turreted steeple, built in 1804. Return and descend the steepish slope by the steps. Carry on along the path through mixed woodland. Where the path divides, take the one nearest to the river. Walk on with care to pass a weir and remain on the path nearest to the hurrying burn. Pass through a gap in a stone wall.

7 Cross a substantial wooden footbridge over the Lednock. Bear right to walk along the track bed of the old railway and follow the path until it meets a lane and the car park.

Wren

Practicals

This pleasing walk starts from an attractive village. It continues upstream of the lovely river through a richly wooded gorge to two dramatic waterfalls. It visits a viewpoint with an enormous monument. Once the river is crossed the return along the glen, much of it wooded, is equally delightful.

Total distance:	4½ miles/7.2km
Time:	3 hours
Map:	OS Landranger 52/Explorer 368
Terrain:	Distinct paths all the way but some can be steep and muddy.

7

Lady Mary's Walk and Laggan Hill, Crieff

Park in Taylor Park, grid ref 858222. To reach this attractive grassy recreation area, drive north-west through the town centre following West High Street. At the junction, turn right, uphill, into Comrie Street. Take the first left into Milnab Street, which leads downhill to Taylor Park and ample parking spaces.

Crieff. In the 17th century Crieff was Perthshire's principal market town. Scotland's largest cattle sales were held here, the animals being driven from all over the Highlands. Many dealers came up from the south and the cattle were then herded on into England along drove roads that today are frequented by walkers. Then the south facing town became a fashionable Victorian health resort. Today it is the bustling 'capital' of Strathearn, the broad valley of the River Earn.

Lady Mary. She was Lady Mary Murray, the daughter of Sir Patrick Murray of Ochtertyre. The walk along the north bank of the River Earn, was created in 1815 by

Lady Mary's Walk, Crieff

Sir Patrick and, because it was his daughter's favourite it was named after her. It also remains one of the favourite walks for the people of Crieff and its visitors.

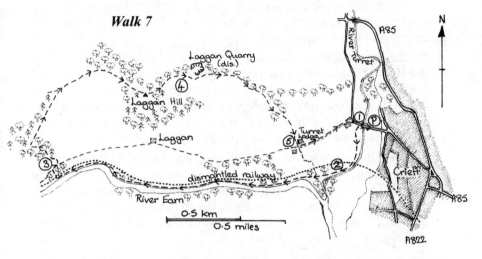

Walk 7

1 Cross the bridge over the fast-flowing River Turret. Beyond, look left for the footpath sign for the walk. Stride along the tree-lined path, with the noisy burn to the left. To the right lie pastures. Pass between the pillars of an old bridge that once carried a railway line over the Turret to Loch Earn and beyond. Notice the embankment to the right where the line continued.

2 Follow the path, which in summer is lined with wood cranesbill, and the aromatic sweet cicely. Pass through a kissing gate and head along the glorious way. It then swings away from the Turret and comes beside the wide, stately River Earn, just west of the confluence. The path soon joins the wide way beneath a row of magnificent beech trees, with some lime, larch and scots pine. The wide, flat, easy-to-walk path continues for a mile, keeping close to the pleasing river, where dippers feed in the rapids and mallards dawdle in the shallows. Walk on where the track becomes a narrow path and follow it where it swings right away from the hurrying water to pass between two pillars of another defunct bridge.

3 At the T-junction of tracks, turn right for a few steps, and then go through a gate on the left to ascend a clear winding path which keeps to the right-hand side of mixed woodland. Where it swings up to the right, follow it to a kissing gate and continue on the edge of woodland with a wire fence on the right. At the next gateway, bear right along a

track coming in from the left. Soon the wooded top of Laggan Hill is reached, marked by a fine old wrought-iron seat, which was no doubt placed there when there was a wide panoramic view of Strathearn. Alas, the now mature conifers below have grown up to obscure the prospect, and walkers must hope for the day when some ruthless tree-felling will open it up again.

4 On the steady descent, there are very pleasant views over Crieff, with the Hydro complex high on the hill opposite, topped by the trees and the viewpoint of The Knock. The entrance to a disused quarry on the left is now so overgrown that you can easily pass it without realizing the extent of the former workings. The track makes its way down towards new houses on the outskirts of the town.

5 On reaching a crossroad, with Turret Lodge on the left corner, and where the track ahead is signposted as another approach to Lady Mary's Walk, turn left along a narrow metalled road, keeping the row of tidy modern houses on your right. Go on to the end, then turn right downhill. Soon you pass the start of your walk, and cross the bridge over the Turret to regain the car park.

Dipper

Practicals

Easy walking, A pleasing leisurely woodland walk beside the River Earn. Your return is over Laggan Hill.

Total distance:	4 miles/6.5km
Time:	2 hours
Maps:	OS Landranger 52/Explorer 368

8

The Knock of Crieff

To reach the car park, grid ref 865226, go up the narrow one-way Hill Street which has signposts for Crieff Hydro and Morrison's Academy. After widening for two-way traffic, the road becomes Ferntower Road. Drive to the top of this road, turn left and then immediately fork right, where there are signs for an intimidating range of Hydro destinations (suites, chalets, stables etc.) but no mention of the Knock. Press on and soon the lower of two car parks is reached.

The Knock is a large Old Red Sandstone mound mainly covered in deciduous woodland. Its name 'Knock' comes from the Gaelic word for hill – 'Cnoic'. It is 793ft/241m high.

1 Walk back a few metres, then go off left along a wide ride, with dense woodland on the left and fine views over Strathearn to the right. Keep along this route, ignoring tracks turning uphill. Soon you reach a new landmark, the Millenium Cairn erected for January 1, 2000. It is built in the beehive shape of a broch. The ruins of Ferntower, a house with an enviable viewpoint, lie to the right.

2 The ride begins to climb and curve left round the hill. After rounding the nose of the hill, follow the waymark to the right, directing you to a narrow track which detours to the right and gives access, over a wire fence, to an outstanding viewpoint. From a raised knoll next to the trunk of a dead conifer, you can look across

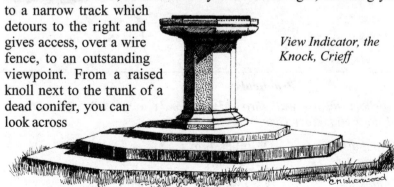

View Indicator, the Knock, Crieff

0.5 km
0.5 miles

N **Walk 8**

Knock of Crieff
Millennium Cairn
Ferntower
Dryton
P
Hydro
Crieff

the valley in which the delightfully named Shaggie Burn winds down between the picturesque hamlet of Monzie and Monzie Castle, and to see the bulk of the nearest Munro, Ben Chonzie, filling the middle distance. Over to the left, a fine panorama of the hills surrounding Strathearn opens out, with Ben More seen in the background on a clear day.

3 Return to the path, go through the trees to the right, and join the main ride for a short distance until a fence and gateway are reached, as the track starts to descend. Here take a left turn along a rising footpath, forking to the right where it divides by another fence.

4 This pleasant, flower bedecked-path leads to the summit of The Knock and a substantial marble memorial plinth. The brass plate it supports identifies the main mountain tops you can see.

5 Leave by the track which continues ahead, westwards, and descends through mainly deciduous woodland to the car park.

Scots pine

Practicals

A short steepish walk through woodland to a splendid viewpoint on Knock Hill above Crieff.

Total distance: 2½ miles/4km
Time: 1–1½ hours
Maps: OS Landranger 52/Explorer 368

9

Tullibardine Chapel and the Birks

Park at Tullibardine chapel, grid ref 909135. To reach this, take the A823 from its junction with the A9 in the direction of Crieff, passing through the extensive Gleneagles hotel, golf and leisure complex. A mile beyond the mini roundabout, a signpost directs right for Tullibardine chapel. Follow the single-track road until it turns right. Go round beyond the chapel where there is space to park on the verge without obstructing farm traffic.

Tullibardine Chapel dates from 1446, when it was erected on the orders of Sir David Murray, then resident at Tullibardine Castle. This castle has now vanished, having been pulled down with its stones taken for use in other buildings. The chapel survived the reformation intact, and is now preserved as an important Ancient Monument.

Tullibardine Chapel

1 Before you set off, it is worthwhile having a look around the well-preserved little chapel. The route for the walk goes through a pedestrian gate on the north-west side of the chapel, follows a fence to the right of the field, then joins a stony farm track which runs gently down to the Buchany Burn and crosses it into a large field. There is a good vista of the Perthshire hills beyond the woodland which is your first objective. Follow the tractor track straight across the field, making for a stand of four Douglas firs. On nearing these, the track swings right and takes you to a gateway by a very dead tree. Beyond, turn sharp left up a ride, which runs the length of the Birks of Tullibardine. Roe deer frequent the plantations on each side, and you are quite likely to see one or more prancing across the track ahead.

2 After just over ½ mile/1km, the track crosses a burn and, on the right, there is an enclosure with various frames used for holding feed for young pheasants. Beyond this, the surface deteriorates for a short distance, with deep ruts usually filled with water. Negotiate this bit as best you can on one side or the other, with a dense conifer plantation on the right hand side. When this plantation recedes from the edge of the track, look for an indistinct path turning right and running between the conifer plantation and the next one. This is almost immediately joined by all-terrain vehicle tracks, which have churned up the ground fairly deeply, but have the advantage of clearly indicating the route. This soon doubles back to the right and crosses more open ground.

3 Soon the ruined buildings of Farmton Muir farm are seen to the right, and the path goes through a gateway into a grassy track, fenced on both sides, which becomes a farm track leading to the main Farmton

Walk 9

buildings. Pass these on the left, cross a bridge over the dismantled railway and go down the ramp on the other side.

4 Here, double back on the right, taking a path across a burn on a little bridge and continuing through a gate which leads to the railway trackbed. Turn left and follow the gently rising way, which in spring is spangled with primroses. Listen for the call of the curlew at nesting time. You may also hear a woodpecker drumming on a tree trunk not far away in the woods. About half-way along the old rail track, you pass through a gate and are joined, from the right, by the ride you walked earlier. The conjoined route goes on in a straight line mainly on an embankment, and eventually, when it starts to curve left, you will see the grounds of the former Tullibardine station house. Reaching its gate, take a well-used path turning off to the right, which goes between fences with substantial railway stonework visible on the left, to join a minor road.

5 Turn right and follow the quiet road until you reach the corner, where you turn right by the chapel to your parked car.

Greater Spotted Woodpecker

Practicals

Type of walk: A pleasant, mainly level circuit through open farmland and woodland, returning along the trackbed of an abandoned railway.

Total distance: 4¼ miles/7km
Time: 2 hours
Maps: OS Landranger 58/Explorer 368

10

A walk in Abernethy Glen

Park in Abernethy's free 'Inn Close' car park, grid ref 190163. This modest space has no signpost from the High Street, and to find it drive from the east side of the town, past the post office and inn. Turn sharp left up a narrow road, then left again into the parking area behind the building from which it takes its name.

Abernethy lies in a fold of the Ochils overlooking the fertile plains of the Earn and the Tay. It is a gracious old town with houses that front onto the street. It was once an important Pictish settlement and it has a well preserved round tower. This was believed to have been constructed in the 9th century. It was used for keeping watch against marauders, as a sanctuary in time of trouble and a place to store valuables and records. A spiral staircase was put in at a later date and a clock added. Look for the metal collar (jougs) used as a pillory for those who infringed church rules. Notice the piece of Pictish sculptured stone at the foot of the tower.

Round Tower, Abernethy

C.M.Isherwood

Witches.
Near the lochan just beyond the

40

hilltop cairn on Castle Law is where local witches were supposed to have held their covens. The hill, Quarrel Knowe, legend tells, is where the witches met to settle their differences. Witches Road, again according to legend, is where women, accused of being witches, were led along for burning on Abernethy Hill (to your left) and where their ashes were scattered.

1 Return to the High Street and turn right to pass the post office. Walk right up narrow Kirk Wynd, where the Abernethy Glen Walk is signposted. Go past a striking church, which at the time of publication is undergoing reconstruction and is set to provide attractive living accommodation. Continue along a lane where, in autumn, the hedgerows are laden with hips, haws and blackberries.

2 Where the road divides take the left branch and go on to where it becomes a track. Follow it as it swings to the right. It passes below Loanhead Quarry, which was used for the production of road metal and chips before the seam ran out in 1942. Now its face is clad with heather and long grass, and trees grow about its top and on any ledge where roots can take hold. Pause on the seat to enjoy the view over the lower Earn valley and then walk on where the slopes to the left are steep and tree-clad. To the right are pastures and the town lies beyond.

3 Follow the path (Witches Road) into deciduous woodland. Below to your right, the Ballo Burn chuckles as it hurries through the trees. Descend rather steep steps to the side of the burn. Continue along the path, beside the stream, and where it begins to climb. Cross duckboards and pass through a gate. Turn right and walk a couple of steps to the road.

4 Turn right and follow the waymark, directing you along the road in the direction of Glenfoot. Look for the sign on the left for Castle Law.

Follow the stony cart track uphill and go on where it swings left and then right, easing the gradient, to a signpost directing you along a path to the summit, from where there are grand views. An iron-age fort here dates from about 500 to 300 B.C. Just beyond is the small lochan which could have supplied the fort and the place where the witches are supposed to have met.

5 Return the same way and turn left to walk the road. Turn right, just after the small hill, Quarrel Knowe. Walk past large gates on your left, belonging to the water board, and continue along a rough track of chippings. It runs through the Rough Glen and was once part of a public road along which were carried great quantities of lime and coal. Climb a ladder stile and continue along the peaceful, tree-lined track.

6 Climb the next ladder stile and from here look for stones in the track that were part of a highway before 1820. Step out along the reinforced track until you reach the road. Turn right and walk in front of Tootie House, where once the cowherd sounded his horn. He alerted people to release their cows so that they could be taken to the common grazing ground. Walk on to the small square with its memorial cross. Here look for the round tower on the left. From here it is just a short walk to the car park.

Bramble and hips

Practicals

Type of walk: Delightful, with pleasing views, along rough ways through the hills behind Abernethy.

Total distance:	3 miles/5km
Time:	2 hours
Maps:	OS Landranger 58/Explorer 370

Kinnoull Hill, east of Perth

Cross the Tay by the northernmost bridge in Perth, from west to east, and drive ahead to climb uphill. Pass the hospital and continue until you see a signpost, directing you right, for Kinnoull Hill Forest Walks. Drive along the narrow road to park in the quarry car park, grid ref 135235, where there is a map of the hill that gives suggestions for walks.

The Summit. The summit cairn tells you that Lord Dewar gave this lovely hill to the city of Perth in 1923. The secondary summit cairn has a view indicator panel, helping you identify the wonderful panorama. Close by is a stone table, rather near to the edge of the sheer cliffs of the hill. From here you can enjoy a glorious view of the River Tay meandering gracefully through its fertile plain, on its way to the sea, and of the motorway bridge. The table was erected by an Earl of Kinnoull, a former proprietor of the hill. Look left from here to see Kinnoull Tower built by the ninth Earl of Kinnoull as a ruin, a fashion of the time, after he had seen the castles of the Rhine on his Grand Tour. Below the Tower you can see Kinfauns Castle, built in 1825 for the Earl of Moray.

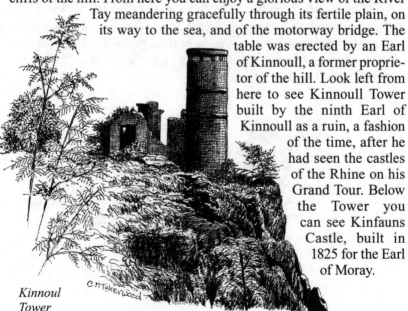

Kinnoul Tower

1 Leave the quarry car park by sturdy wooden steps. These lead to a wide grassy track signed to 'Summit' which climbs steadily through pleasing deciduous woodland. Many small tracks lead off the main one but ignore these and head for the heights. The track ascends through birch, with a glorious carpet of heather and bilberry. Follow the track straight up the hill until it joins a larger track on which you bear right.

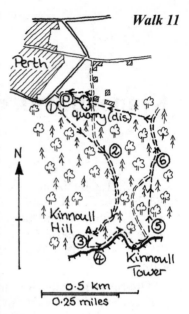

2 Follow the wide way as it swings to the right, to pass through more woodland, passing another 'Summit' sign on the way. The route rises steadily, then drops for a short distance before rising again, more steeply, through broom bushes. Ahead lies the trig point, bench seats and the two view cairns.

3 Walk on from the summit to the secondary summit with the stone table, more bench seats, and wide views over the Tay valley.

4 Turn left and follow the path down through woodland with a glimpse of the tower through the trees. At the bottom of the short descent, follow the track round to the right and climb up to the tower with more views across the wide strath below.

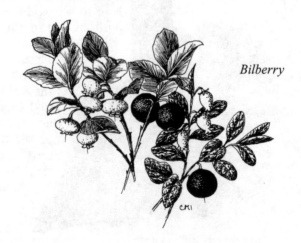

Bilberry

44

5 To return, take the path which goes into the woods directly away from the cliff edge, signed 'Nature Walk'. The path rises slightly and then descends through beautiful mixed pine and deciduous woodland with rowan, hazel and birch. Follow the path through a small stand of thick conifers to join a larger path.

6 Continue downhill through open pine then larch woodland to a path junction. Turn left following the sign to 'Quarry Car Park'. Cross a dry ditch and bear right on a clear path through the woods, with glimpses of open fields beyond. Where several path converge bear right towards a group of houses. Follow the path outside the garden hedges to emerge on an open hillside with a viewpoint and picnic tables. Enjoy the wide views over the city of Perth, then take the left-most path down the hill to the road at the entrance to the quarry car park.

Wild raspberries

Practicals

Type of walk: A pleasing short walk with great rewards along the way and from the summit.

Total distance:	2 miles/3.2km
Time:	1 hour
Maps:	OS Landranger 58/Explorer 369

12

Standing Stone and Stone Circle on the moors above Fowlis Wester and on to Loch Meallbrodden

To park at grid ref 930250, head north-east from Crieff to Gilmerton. Continue on the A85 to New Fowlis. Then turn left up through Fowlis Wester and Pitlandy and left again to the parking area.

Fowlis Wester. The village is very small. Almost all of it can be seen from the square. It is difficult to believe that in 1794 the population was over a thousand and the village had two butchers, several tailors and many shoemakers and smiths. There were shops and inns and numerous weavers and farmers. It is equally difficult to believe that the main route to Perth passed through the small gap between the church and the post office.

Close by the square is the magnificent **church of St Bean**. St Bean was an 8th-century Irish missionary, grandson of the King of Leinster.

Standing stones and stone circle, Braes of Fowlis

There has been a church on this site for more than a thousand years. The present church dates from the 13th century and is well worth a visit.

The square is dominated by a **Pictish cross slab** of weathered red sandstone dating from the eighth or ninth century. Look for carvings on the stone and an iron ring. The stone was used as a pillory and miscreants were chained to it and pelted with eggs.

Standing Stone and Stone Circle. The magnificent bronze age standing stone and the remains of the stone circle are seen on the moors above Fowlis Wester. Alas many of the stones of the circle were removed in the 19th century and used for house and wall building.

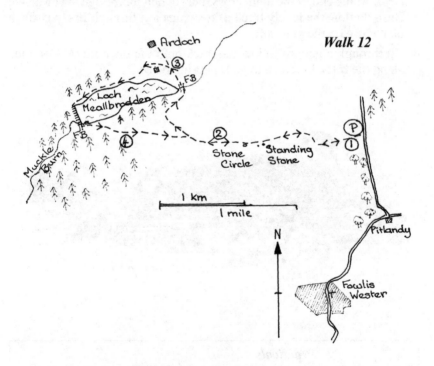

1 After closing the gate beyond the parking area, walk ahead along the track that crosses the moorland. In late August the way passes through a great mass of heather. Leave the track just before a derelict building and walk left to see the standing stone. Close by it are the remains of the stone circle. What a wonderful view our ancestors had from this ridge moor.

47

2 Continue along the track, where grouse feed on heather shoots, and follow it as it begins to descend gently. At the junction, take the right branch and continue along the side of a conifer plantation. Cross a wide footbridge over a small stream and walk on. To the left lies little Loch Meallbrodden, a delightful expanse of water with deciduous trees to the right and a plantation of conifers beyond. The loch is the haunt of mallard and these alight and take off with much splashing.

3 Pass through the gate on the left in the fence, just before a huge ash. Walk ahead, keeping to the right of a farm barn. Stroll along the path, which keeps close to the loch. Climb the stile and walk on. Cross the loch's overflow, wading if necessary, to walk along the dam at its head. At the end of the dam, cross the wooden footbridge over Muckle Burn. Follow the lovely track as it swings left through firs, passing a boathouse on the your left.

4 Go through a gate to follow the track onto the open moor. Continue along the track to return to your parking place.

Mallard and kingcups

Practicals

Type of walk: A delightful quiet walk across seemingly remote moorland to a pretty loch. Easy walking but expect plenty of mud after rain.

Total distance:	2½ miles/4km
Time:	1½ hours
Maps:	OS Landranger 52 or 58/Explorer 368

Glen Lochay

Park in the large space at the end of the metalled road just beyond Kenknock, grid ref 466365. To reach this use either of the minor roads which leave the A827 either side of the River Lochay just north of Killin.

Glen Lochay is a short but beautiful glen, the centre of the old hunting forest of Mamlorn. Its wooded lower reaches soon give way to the lonely, relatively remote upper glen, where this walk is set. It is the start of the climb to five Munros. It is bleak on a dull day but, in good weather, the views in both directions and the sense of isolation make this walk thoroughly enjoyable.

Glen Lochay and Ben Challum

1 Walk straight ahead from the car park to cross a bridge and on through a gate. The track, which is old and pleasant to walk, runs along the riverbank and under a huge pipe, part of the local hydro scheme. Where the path forks take the right branch which leads away from the river towards a barn on the hillside. Go through the

1 km
1 mile

gate beside the barn and wind round hummocks of moraine before coming downhill to the riverbank once more. At the head of the glen you can see dramatic Ben Challum. The track winds round between a stand of conifers and the river. Dippers frequent this fast upland burn and buzzards soar over the surrounding hillsides. To your right is bulky Beinn Heasgarnich with the more interesting rocky spurs of Creag Mhor beyond towards the head of the glen. Across the river are first Sgiath Chuil and then Meall Glas, both rather undistinguished from this side. In autumn deer wander the lower slopes and the roaring of the stags is with you all day.

Red deer stag

2 Go along the track below the farm buildings of Badour and on towards the cottage at Batavaime. Go up, right, towards the dwelling to go across the bridge over the Allt Batavaim. Once over, the

track curves round and begins to climb the hillside towards one of the spurs of Creag Mhor – Sron nan Eun (the bird's nose). At a fork take the right branch which zigzags gently on uphill. There is an obvious old spoil heap ahead and above this your track joins a hydro track.

3 Turn right and, after a little climbing, the way contours along the side of the glen. Continue on the easy way, crossing the many burns by bridges. The views down the glen are splendid, towards Meall nan Tarmachan and the fertile flat bottomed Glen Lochay with deciduous woods on either side and in the distance a glimpse of Loch Tay. Go through a gate and carry on along the high level way.

4 Eventually you come to another spoil heap and then cross the pipeline. There is a locked gate across the track beyond this point so you will have to climb the wooden fence beside it to reach the tarred hydro road from Kenknock over to Glen Lyon. Turn right and descend the zigzags to return to the parking space.

Heath milkwort

Practicals

Type of walk: An easy walk on tracks all the way, with splendid views in good weather. For deer shooting information (26 Aug–20 Oct), use Glen Dochart and Glen Lochay Hillphones Service (recorded message) 01567 820886.

Total distance:	7½ miles/12km
Time:	3–4 hours
Maps:	OS Landranger 51/Explorer 378

14

Sron a'Chlachain from Killin

Killin has several car parks. This walk starts from one at grid ref 573326. To access this, if coming from the south by the A827, cross the bridge over the River Dochart and turn right. The car park for 40 cars lies 77yds/70m along on the right. If this is full there are larger ones further on through the town, but you will have to adapt the walk.

Moirlanich Longhouse is a rare surviving example of a traditional longhouse where people lived in one end and their animals in the other. It is built with crucks and would have had a thatched roof.

In the 15th century the Campbells of Breadalbane bought the Auchmore lands from the MacNabs, including **Finlarig Castle**. This became their headquarters and also the place where they beheaded prisoners for whom they were unable to extract a ransom.

Moirlanich Longhouse

Walk 14

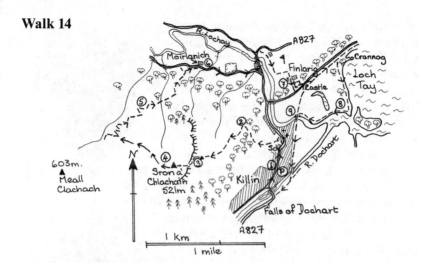

1 Return to the main road from the car park and turn right. Walk through the pleasant town to pass the primary school on the left. Shortly after this turn left through a gate into Breadalbane Park. Turn left again on the first path, which runs up the edge of the grass. At the top of the park go through the gate into the pasture beyond and continue straight ahead up the slope. Bear left at a vague Y-junction and then climb up a broad grassy swathe through the bracken-covered top of the field. Climb a ladder stile over the fence into open mature oak woodland and follow the path as it bears right to traverse the wood.

2 Near the top of the trees the path turns sharply left and then continues for a short distance just above the trees before it swings right and crosses open ground. Pass under the power line and start to climb steeply. From now on there are several steep climbs interspersed with level bits where you can get your breath back. Eventually you arrive on a small summit with rocky outcrops and a superb view back over Loch Tay to Ben Lawers and Meall nan Tarmachan. Then go slightly downhill to cross a damp area and climb the grassy slope beyond. In summer this is colourful with lady's alpine mantle, common speedwell and tormentil.

3 Wind through a gully in low cliffs. Cross another level area and then walk up a fairly gentle slope, with an old wall on your left, until you reach a cairn at the start of the summit plateau. Continue across this to an even more substantial cairn, which marks the actual summit. Here you will want to pause again to enjoy the view. You can now see Ben More and Stobinian up Glen Dochart behind the shoulder of Meall a'Clachach, the highest point of the hill you are on.

4 Bear right as you leave the summit, heading north-west for a small rise on the edge of Glen Lochay. Cross above the start of a burn and descend the hillside a little way but do not go down onto the steeper lower slopes. There is a sloping grassy shelf below the grassy top of the hillside, with many animal tracks along it. Contour along one of these, aiming for a clump of larch trees on a cliffside ahead. The walking is easy and the grass full of heath spotted orchids in the late spring. Before reaching the trees you will notice a path coming towards you down the slope; it is more of a groove than a path and is the line of an old peat road, which came up from Glen Lochay to the peat cuttings on top of the hill. Aim for this path and join it at an obvious hairpin bend, and then zigzag down the hillside on it, or beside it, checking the line if ever it becomes less obvious. In many places it has walls of stone and turf beside it and is very clear.

5 Cross a fence and go through a gap in the old stone wall, beyond. Then continue across the top of a pasture, ford a burn and wind down through another field. At the bottom go through a gate and on down the next field. The minor road up Glen Lochay comes into view and also a house with a red corrugated iron roof. This is Moirlanich Longhouse, owned by the National Trust for Scotland. Where the track curves away to the left, low down the field, turn right and follow a tractor track which heads towards the longhouse. Go through a gate in the electrified deer fence opposite, taking care to avoid rucksacks touching the high electric wires above the gate.

6 Look at the Longhouse and then turn right and walk ½mile/1km down the minor road to Bridge of Lochay, where there is an inn. Turn left on the main road and cross the narrow bridge, with care. A hundred metres

Melancholy thistle

54

beyond the bridge, turn right into
the entrance to a golf course and
walk past the clubhouse and
on down a pleasing level
track. There is a wall to
the left with mature trees
beside it. Turn left with
the track, now grassy,
to walk through
an avenue of tall
sycamores and, at
the end, turn right
over a small bridge,
signed 'Finlarig Castle
and Pier Road'. Go through
the kissing gate beyond, and on
down the farmtrack between the
cottage and farm buildings to reach
a road. Turn right and walk past the
ruins of the castle, which stands in
trees to your left. This is privately owned
and in a dangerous state so you enter at your own
risk, but you can walk up a path through the trees to look at the ruins
from a short distance without incurring danger.

Stonechats

7   Return to the road and go downhill to join the pier road at the bottom
and turn left. The way runs down to the old pier on Loch Tay, which
was also served by a railway. Two hundred metres along, the road and
the railway converge. Here go through a gap in the bushes to walk along
the path on the railway, now a walkway. Ahead Loch Tay becomes
visible through the trees but, before you reach it, take a kissing gate
on the right to walk a path running along behind the shore. At first it
is separated from the shore by a great swathe of iris. The easy way
soon comes closer to the loch as it continues on a sandy embankment.
There are wonderful views over the loch, to the left and, to the right,
the hill you have already climbed. Look back up the loch side to a
tree-covered crannog, its causeway made visible by rooted rushes and
willows in the shallow water covering it.

8   Turn right with the path, where the river enters the loch, and go through
another kissing gate to follow the river bank which, in early summer, is
lined with melancholy thistles and meadowsweet. Another gate leads
into a pasture, with ahead, a splendid view of Meall nan Tarmachan.

Carry on until the path winds round and climbs the bank onto the old railway trackbed again.

9 Turn left and cross the bridge over the Lochay. Stroll on along the railway line. The path ends at a road in a new housing estate. Go straight ahead and where the road swings right take a path on the left to rejoin the railway track once more. Cross the River Dochart on a high bridge and swing right to walk through mature beech above the foaming water. Come down to join a track where you turn right. Walk on between two houses to come out through imposing gateposts to reach the main road. Turn right and cross the bridge, with care, below the spectacular Falls of Dochart. Turn right at the far end of the bridge and return seventy metres to the car park.

Wood vetch

Practicals

Type of walk: Careful navigation required to find the path down the steep hill. Easy and delightful by Loch Tay and the rivers. Very varied walk, views superb. See information on deer stalking in Walk 13 'Practicals'.

Total distance:	6–6½ miles/10.4km
Time:	4 hours
Maps:	OS Landranger 51/Explorer 378

15

Ben Lawers, Loch Tay

Park at the Visitor Centre, grid ref 609379, operated by the National Trust for Scotland (NT).

Ben Lawers (3984ft/1214m) is the highest mountain in Perthshire. Its summit and southern slopes are owned by the National Trust, which has preserved its famous arctic-alpine flora, for the benefit of the public and for scientific research.

This flora thrives on the mountain's unique soil, a soft, lime-rich schist. The area has always been popular with botanists. It was 'discovered' in 1790 and was a mecca for alpine botanists, collectors and alpine gardeners. In more recent times the pressure has eased and now people like to take photographs of plants rather than pick them.

The 8,000 acre property – Ben Lawers – was bought by the Trust in 1950 using some of the Mountainous Country Fund much of which was bequeathed by Percy Unna (1878-1950). He was President of the Scottish Mountaineering Club and it was through his farsightedness and his generosity that the Trust was able to obtain other mountain properties including Glencoe, Kintail, Goat Fell, Torridon and the Grey Mare's Tail (Moffat).

Meall Corranaich, Ben Lawers and Beinn Ghlas

Scottish Blackface Sheep. These were originally from the Borders and were brought into Perthshire about 1800. Some of the sheep stay on the hill ground all the winter and when it is snow-covered the animals have to scrape the snow away to find food. Although the Trust owns the ground some farms below the Trust's have the right to graze a certain number of sheep on the hill for nothing. Farmers' traditional grazing rights were maintained as a condition of the sale of the land.

1 Leave the car park by the signposted footpath. In the wetter areas look for a plethora of moisture-loving plants. Climb the stile in the deer and sheep fence. Continue along the well-maintained path, enjoying fine views down to Loch Tay. Cross the Burn of Edramucky and climb steadily towards a gate in the fence.

2 From now on you will see the Scottish Blackface sheep grazing. Go on over level moorland and

Lochan na Cat

Allt a' Chobhair

Shielings

④ ▲ Ben Lawers 1214m

③

▲ 1069m
Meall Corranaich

Coire Odhar

▲ Beinn Ghlas 1103m.

1 km
1 mile

Lochan na Lairige

Burn of Edramucky

⑤

②

N

Walk 15

P C
Visitor Centre

then scale several large steepish hummocks to reach the summit of Beinn Ghlas (1103m/3657ft). Beyond, the path slopes gently down before continuing as an airy ridge walk between two corries. Head across a short shoulder, where to the right lies a small lochan.

3 Then begins the steep and fairly lengthy climb to the summit. The path, rocky and rough in places, is easy to follow – some scrambling is required over several more rocky humps. Look in spring on the rocks for purple saxifrage or, a little later, for moss campion. At the top stands a trig point and a

cairn. The views from here are magnificent. You can spot the major peaks of Perthshire and sometimes the Atlantic and the North Sea.

4 Leave the summit and return to the small lochan. Here you may wish to retrace your outward route. This walk takes a path to the right, off the ridge route, following it as it contours the side of Beinn Ghlas, passing below a corrie. Look back down Gleann Da-Eig, through which meanders the Allt Glean Da-Eig, to Glen Lyon far below. The path, occasionally waymarked, passes easily through a tumble of boulders where fir club moss thrives. Then it joins an old track coming up from shielings in Glean Da-Eig and crossing the col between Beinn Ghlas and Meall Corranaich. Continue down this and soon the Visitor Centre comes into view.

5 On reaching your outward route just before the stile, turn right and walk downhill.

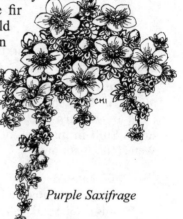

Purple Saxifrage

Practicals

Type of walk: This is an exciting walk but not one to be taken lightly. Care is needed and it should only be undertaken by those with walking boots, waterproofs and hill walking experience. Do not attempt in the mist and turn back if mist descends.

Total distance:	7 miles/11.4km; there and back: over 2,500ft (800m) of ascent
Time:	5–6 hours
Map:	OS Landranger 51/Explorer 378

16

Falls of Acharn

Leave your car in the parking area, grid ref 756438, close to the sign-posted start of the walk.

Dorothy Wordsworth's comments, in 1803, on her visit to the Falls of Acharn are reported by Louis Stott in his book of Scottish Waterfalls as follows:

> We entered a dungeon-like passage and, after walking some yards in total darkness found ourselves in a quaint apartment stuck over with moss, hung about with stuffed foxes and ornamented with a library of wooden books covered with old leather backs, the mock furniture of a hermit's cell. At the end of the room, through a large bow window, we saw the waterfall, and at the same time looking down to the left, the village of Kenmore and part of the lake – a very beautiful prospect.

The **Burn of Acharn** gathers its waters from a large area below Sron a' Chaoineidh. It then tumbles down a hanging valley to enter Loch Tay close to Acharn Point and west of Kenmore.

Falls of Acharn

The last glaciers retreated from these parts about 10,000 years ago leaving flat-bottomed, steep-sided, U-shaped valleys. The main valley of the Tay was deepened more than the smaller tributary valleys. Waterfalls are a feature of these hanging valleys where side streams, such as the Acharn, drop down steep slopes to reach the main valley.

1 From the parking area, head up the reinforced track. Look back often to see Loch Tay overlooked by Drummond Hill. To the west lies Ben Lawers. As you climb, the river is lost to sight, deep in its gorge, but the sound of its descent fills the air.

Walk 16

2 Follow the signpost for the Hermit's Cave, a folly, and walk through a dark tunnel to a railed platform for a wonderful view of the falls, where the burn descends over stepped ledges of flaggy Dalradian rocks. Then the raging water drops for many feet in a curtain of white lace, divided near its base by a projecting boulder. The resultant twin falls hurtle into a dark brown pool. Next, the water is imprisoned by the sides of a narrow ravine before raging into a second pool. From here it slides to the left at right angles to the main fall before it plummets deeper into the glen. Miss Wordsworth would have been more impressed if she could have stood out on the railed platform.

3 Return through the tunnel and turn left to continue. Follow the curving path around the top of the ravine beneath lofty beech. Here a signboard directs you left to a viewing area. This is a walkway and footbridge constructed from timber by Royal Engineers in 1989. It provides and excellent view of the upper falls. The racing burn tumbles over rocks, scouring out cavities and undermining the sides of the narrow gorge. While standing on the bridge, close to the walls of the gorge, look for the many ferns, mosses and lichens growing here.

4 Do not cross the bridge but return to the main track and continue up the to the High Bridge – a traditional stone structure giving a good view down the canyon scoured out by the churning waters. To descend, go through a kissing gate and down the path on the right bank of the burn. After negotiating more of the sappers' wooden steps and bridgework, pause at a convenient seat on a rocky outcrop for a view across to the Hermit's Cave, with Ben Lawers in the background.

5 Continue downhill to the end of the track, where there is an old water-mill, now a private house. A few steps, left over the road bridge, takes you back to your car.

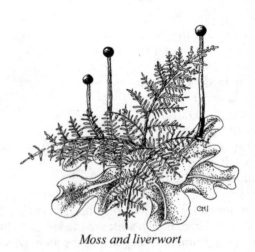

Moss and liverwort

Practicals

Type of walk: A dramatic ascent and descent beside a raging burn along good footpaths, with exciting viewing platforms and walkways to obtain the best views. Easy underfoot as you climb and descend but strong footwear required.

Total distance:	1½ miles/2.5km
Time:	1 hour
Map:	OS Landranger 52/Explorer 378

17

The Birks of Aberfeldy and the Falls of Moness

Visitors to Aberfeldy are given every encouragement to explore the Birks (old Scots for birches) and the wonderful waterfalls on the Moness Burn. There are two free car parks off the A826 Aberfeldy–Crieff road (clearly signposted on the right if coming from the centre of town). The top one, grid ref 855485, is more convenient and has a dispenser offering a useful leaflet about the nature trail. In the unlikely event of the space being full, drive back a few metres to the lower park and walk back up.

Den. In the Scottish dialect 'den' means 'a wooded glen', an apt description for the Den of Moness.

Robert Burns visited in 1787 and is said to have composed his song "The Birks o' Aberfeldy" sitting on a rocky ledge overlooking the fall. This is now known as Robert Burns's seat.

Birch Trees. The birch is the most common tree to be found at the highest part of the walk. Birch produces vast quantities of small winged seeds, which are easily dispersed by the wind. Where the ground has been disturbed the birch can colonise readily and is fast growing, taking advantage of the lack of competition.

Burns's seat

1 Start the walk from the car park and, when the track divides, ignore the signs for the left fork. This is your return route. Go straight ahead, keeping to the west bank of the burn. The way passes beneath magnificent beech trees. Gradually the gorge deepens and you can no longer see the burn – only hear it raging on its way.

2 Continue on, climbing higher and higher, until the path passes beneath birch. Take a pause on a convenient seat before carrying on up the path. Cross a small bridge and take a longer pause on the next seat from where there is a magnificent view of the Perthshire hills. The noise of the Moness increases but not a glimpse of the falls is yet to be seen. Peer over the protective fence at the sheer sides of the gorge. When you reach a fork, go down left to cross the bridge over the spectacular falls. Though they rage and roar, it is still difficult to see their full magnificence.

Walk 17

3 From the bridge, climb again to continue up steps. Then begin your descent of a series of steps to a wonderful viewpoint, where the Falls of Moness can be seen in all their glory. The burn drops in three great white-topped falls, crashing over ledges and plunging into pools and a continual noise resounds from this dramatic hollow. Spray fills the air and covers the luxuriant vegetation. Birch, larch and scots pine line the sides of the gorge.

4 Follow the path as it zig-zags down, dropping rapidly, well stepped and railed. Look for the pretty wood vetch flourishing here. Continue ahead to another viewing point where the burn comes down in innumerable cascades before descending in one long jet into a very deep pool. The sides of the gorge flare upwards. The rock face beside the viewpoint is dripping with water and here liverworths thrive, together with the fragile feather, fork and hair mosses. In spring vast sheets of golden saxifrage brighten the ravine.

5 Return and continue your descent along a pleasingly constructed wooden walkway. Cross the next bridge, from where you can almost touch a graceful fall, on a tributary burn. Stroll along the path to see yet another side fall which rages down rocky ledges to join the Moness. Follow the path down to see the burn's final plummeting descent. Look for Robert Burns' seat as you walk on.

6 Carry on the stepped way to pass yet another fall and then go on along another very satisfying wooden way, built by sappers in 1986. Finally you reach the bed of the ravine, with its tree-clad sides towering overhead. The path goes on over the Moness and returns you to the upper car park.

Silver birch

Practicals

Type of walk: A magical walk, particularly on the descent, to view another of Perthshire's many glorious waterfalls.

Total distance:	2 miles/3.4km
Time:	2 hours
Map:	OS Landranger 52/Explorer 379
Terrain:	The path is rough in places and runs along steep slopes where young children should be kept under control at all times. Sturdy footwear essential, particularly after wet weather.

18

Loch Freuchie and Glen Almond

Park in one of two big laybys in the "Sma' Glen", on the A822 road between Gilmerton and Amulree, grid ref 889314. This is just south of Newton Bridge, where the road crosses the River Almond.

Wade Roads To facilitate movement of government troops in the Scottish Highlands during the 18th century, General Wade embarked on the construction of a network of military roads connecting the garrisons. This was the first long-distance road building programme undertaken in Scotland since the Roman occupation. The courses of several Wade Roads are still followed by modern motor roads, including that through the central section of the "Sma' Glen".

Loch Freuchie or Fraoch – the heathery loch. The loch, a long stretch of silvery water, fills a quiet hollow in Glen Quaich. Half way down the loch is one small island covered with pines. This is a crannog, a prehistoric man-made island. Legend has it that a young lover, Fraoch braved a dragon that dwelt there to obtain rowan berries for his lady, Maidh. He successfully completed his task having evaded the dragon. But Maidh insisted that she wanted the tree as well. So he returned but on uprooting it, disturbed the dragon. During the ensuing fight the dragon gnawed off Fraoch's limbs but he still managed to slay the beast. Maidh found both lying dead on the shore of the crannog.

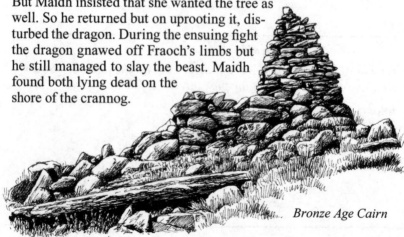

Bronze Age Cairn

c.M. Isherwood

1 Go carefully beside the road northwards across Newton Bridge and round a bend to the right. Just before the plantation on the right ends, leave the road by a gate on the left and cross a stone bridge. Looking right, you can see the original Wade road going straight ahead up a slight rise. Reach it by negotiating a boggy area by the least uncomfortable route, and follow the track until it joins an estate track coming down from the left and then returns to the A822 through a gate.

2 Walk the road with care for about ¼ mile/0.4km as far as a layby on the left. Go through a gate just beyond and start up the track ahead for a few paces, then turn right over a knoll following tractor tracks. These take you through a gateway, across a burn and on up the field, with a wire fence on the left and scots pine sheltering Corrymuckloch house over to the right, to a wooden gate at the corner. By passing through this gate and a tubular steel one immediately on the left and then winding to the right, with old farm buildings on the right, you regain the course of the Wade Road. Soon you reach a white radio mast. Here, fork left up a more-used track, following the pylons. As it descends, Loch Freuchie is seen ahead. On reaching the single-track road coming up from Amulree, turn left to follow the road for about 1½ mile/2.0km with minimal motor traffic. After a bend, you reach the sign for Croft Mill, on the left.

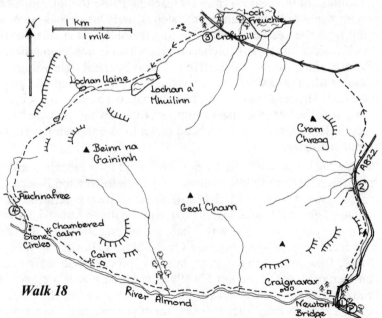

Walk 18

3 Turn up here past the house and continue up the steadily rising track, bearing left when it forks. Although at the time of writing it is not signposted, you are now following the Rob Roy Way long-distance path. The walking is easy up to Lochan a'Mhuillinn, the first lochan in the aptly named Glen Lochan. There is a small dam, probably built to provide a water supply to the now defunct mill. After reaching a fishing hut, the track ends and becomes a narrow path which soon becomes distinctly boggy. Look out for

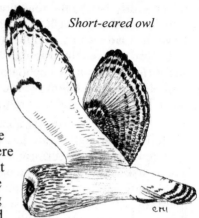

Short-eared owl

a route across the burn to the left, with the path working its stony and heather-girt way up the glen, with the burn below on the right. The next lochan, Lochan Uaine, has been virtually drained and is almost completely covered with reeds. Eventually, the narrow path crosses the burn by a miniature lochan, fed by a slightly bigger one above. Beyond, the summit of the bealach (pass) is reached. Pause to look around and you may spot red deer roaming the slopes, and black grouse may well erupt from the heather nearby. Starting down the other side, the path divides. Keep to the left (higher) route, which is hard going because of encroaching heather on the flank of Sron Bealaidh. The Munro Ben Chonzie fills the skyline above the buildings of Auchnafree below in the valley. Descending steadily, the path meets an estate track coming down from the left by a gate. Go through to follow the grassy track and when it divides, take the right bend down to join the reinforced track from Auchnafree.

4 Double back left along the road, soon joined by a branch coming in from the right, and follow it all the way back to Newton Bridge. The trudge down a long and fairly hard-surfaced road is relieved by the delightful green hillsides, and the sound of the River Almond, the latter accompanying you all the way. There are several sites of both ancient and recent interest along the route. On the right, soon after the junction, is the Millennium Stone Circle, built by a local stone craftsman to commemorate the year 2000. Shortly afterwards, a well-preserved tall bronze-age cairn is seen on the left. Nearer the end of the glen, just before a gravelly bank backed by a plantation is reached, the remaining walls of the settlement of Craignavar can be seen up the slope on the left. They are well worth a diversion if you are interested in seeing the relics of a community expelled in the 19th century clearances. When the track reaches the A822 road, you have only to re-cross the bridge to reach the layby where you have parked.

Red deer

19

Dunkeld, Lowes Nature Reserve, the Hermitage and the Rumbling Bridge, by the River Braan

I Park in the lovely town of Dunkeld, grid ref 025426, and walk from here through Cathedral Street, past houses well restored by the National Trust and Perth County Council. Go through the huge wrought-iron gates of the cathedral. To the left lawns, with scattered trees, slope gently to the banks of the wide, stately Tay. To the right lies the ruined cathedral.

The Cathedral. It took nearly 200 years to complete (1312-1501). In 1560, after the Reformation, it was largely destroyed. Today the restored choir area serves as the parish church. Enjoy the peace to be found within. Look for the 9th century Pictish Apostles' Stone on the right as you enter the Chapter House museum. Behind the carved oak screen, see the recumbent figure of Alexander Stewart, Earl of Badenoch, who lived at Garth Castle. Read the page from the Book of Ruth in the Great 'She' Bible printed in 1611.

II Park at the Loch of Lowes Nature Reserve, grid ref 041436, and then pass through the Visitor Centre to two bird hides.

Ospreys. Use the binoculars and telescopes provided to view the ospreys in their nests atop the pines. The adult birds make excursions to the loch to fish and bathe. Look for tufted duck, great crested grebe, coot, pochard and goosander idling on the lovely stretch of water.

Osprey

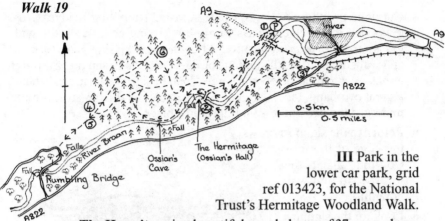

III Park in the lower car park, grid ref 013423, for the National Trust's Hermitage Woodland Walk.

The Hermitage is a beautiful wooded area of 37 acres alongside the River Braan, which here descends in several waterfalls, rapids and cascades. The woodland was created in the 18th century by the Dukes of Atholl as a wild tree garden.

1 Buy a leaflet at the start to enhance your walk. Leave the parking area by the waymarked route behind the board, which gives information about the Hermitage. At waymark 3 you pass below a stand of enormous Douglas fir. At waymark 5 you continue beneath silver fir to a wooden fence. From here look across the river, dark and brooding, to what is reputed to be the tallest tree in Britain, a Douglas fir well over 200ft/62m.

2 Cross the 18th century bridge, spanning a narrow gorge where the River Braan cuts through a rocky ravine below the Black Linn fall. Continue along the woodland way that leads off left on the far side of the river. It climbs high above the hurrying burn. Look back for a grand view of the waterfall bridge. Press on until you reach a gate on to the road. Here if you wish you can head downhill to Inver and along the A9 for a very short distance back to the car park.

3 To continue with this walk, retrace your steps to the bridge and cross. Enter the Hermitage Folly or Ossian's Hall, built in 1758 by the future third Duke of Atholl. From the balcony there is a dramatic view of the falls. Walk further along the waymarked trail. Just beyond waymark 10, look for Ossian's Cave, which like the Hermitage is a romantic folly. Beyond the cave follow the narrow path through the trees, still within sound of the burn. At the next waymark, continue ahead to walk through more conifer woodland. Follow the path as it swings to the left and climbs uphill.

4 Continue in the direction of the signposted Rumbling Bridge. Cross a wooden footbridge to pass through a kissing gate. Walk the wide grassy track over open pasture. After the next kissing gate, turn left and walk downhill to the famous bridge. Here the Braan rages through a rocky canyon far below the single-span bridge. As it surges beneath a great overhang, the noise echoes or rumbles as if from an enormous underground cavern. It is an impressive place.

5 Return to the signpost on the edge of the forest. Continue ahead to a forest road and walk downhill.

6 Look for the signpost to the Hermitage. Follow the directions to the right into the trees then bear left to follow the waymarks leading back to the car park.

The Hermitage (Ossian's Hall), Dunkeld

Practicals

Type of walk: This charming walk takes you through magnificent woodland about the River Braan. It visits two romantic 18th century follies and crosses a fine bridge where the Braan is at its most impressive.

Total distance:	5 miles/8km
Time:	3 hours
Maps:	OS Landranger 52/Explorer 379

Glen Garr and Craig Obney

Leave the A9, close to Dunkeld, by the A822 in the direction of Crieff. After two miles, look for a turn on the right, signposted Rumbling Bridge. Go down the lane and use one of the ample parking areas on the right, grid ref. 997411.

Rumbling Bridge. If you have time to spare and have not already seen the sight (it forms the climax of walk 19, approached from the Hermitage, downstream) it is well worth the few minutes it takes, to follow the track to the bridge and look into the dramatic chasm, with the waters of the River Braan crashing noisily below.

1   From the parking area follow the instructions for the start of the Braan Walk, which initially takes the same route as the Glen Garr walk. The way takes you through oak woodland and across a footbridge. Beyond, turn right to reach the A822, which you cross to walk on up the wide farm track opposite, signposted Glen Garr. Just before the second cattle grid a track leads left for Tomgarrow, which you ignore. Continue climbing gently. Look left to see a lochan sparkling in the sunshine. This is where the Inchewan Burn, seen on walk 21 originates. Ahead lies Birnam Hill, with the cairn on King's Seat, perched on its heather-clad mound, seen on the same walk.

Cairns – remains of old fort, Craig Obney

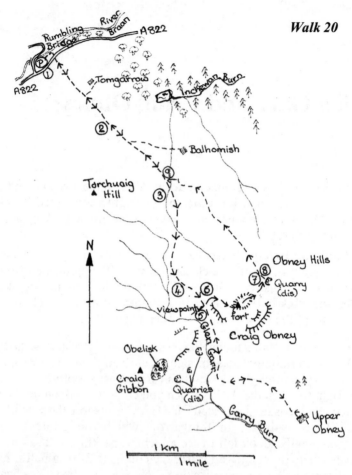

2 Cross another cattle grid and walk ahead to take a signposted grassy track for Glen Garr and Bankfoot, continuing between derelict walls. Then, where the track winds off left to Balhomish farm, climb the stile and go on over pasture. Here you might hear curlews call and then see them take flight. Beyond the next two stiles the track leads into glorious heather moorland.

3 Walk the path as it moves into a wetter area, where bog rosemary grows, and cross two small streams on conveniently placed stones. Pass beneath a solitary pine. Away to the right stands Craig Gibbon, topped with scots pine. The path climbs steadily through mixed bracken and heather. Birches dot the hillside on the lower slopes of the Obney Hills, which lie to the left.

4 Stride along the lovely high-level path. Soon after passing a clump of birch on the right, look out for a narrow path to the right leading, after a few steps, to a promontory overlooking the steep-sided glen. From this fine viewpoint Glen Garr opens up beneath you, with the Garry Burn winding down through the trees. The clear remains of an old light railway track can be seen leading ahead, straight down the valley below the spoil heaps of a now defunct quarry, which it once served. The quarry took slate from the steep rocky side of Craig Gibbon, now straight across from where you stand.

5 Return to the main track and at this point a decision must be made whether to continue down the pleasantly graded route to where it ends at Upper Obney farm and then returning to Rumbling Bridge the way you came. Or, to take a more strenuous circuit, climbing the steep slope ahead of you to the summit of Craig Obney, with its prehistoric fort and wonderful views. If the latter is your choice then this is the way this walk continues.

6 On returning to the main track from the Glen Garr viewpoint, go straight across the track and up the slope passing through mixed bracken and heather. There are faint traces of a path but this peters out as you reach solid heather up the slope. Make your way over to the right towards higher ground through the boot tangling sweetly perfumed plant. Deer trods and slate outcrops make the going marginally easier. Continue on steadily climbing to the trig point. Pause on the pleasing summit, with its well-proportioned cairn, and look for the fascinating circle of stones forming the outline of an ancient fort. Enjoy the glorious views. In the foreground to the west, look for the obelisk on the summit of Craig Gibbon, circled by pines. This structure is marked on the map, but it was obscured by trees when walking the glen path below.

Heather

7 The descent uses an estate track serving shooting butts. Once it led to a quarry whose remains, if you walk over to the eastern ramparts of the fort, are clearly visible on the hillside below. This track is your descent route and it can be seen starting on the broad col to the left of the quarry. Head towards this by going steadily down through the heather on your left. Go carefully down the hillside, which is at first steep, with rocky outcrops. Some of the deer trods are useful,

CHl

providing relief from walking on the springy heather tufts. There is a good chance of seeing a group of red deer leaping away as you head for the track.

8 When you reach the track, turn left and follow it for a mile and a half until it swings left and ends abruptly at a farm gate. Here go down left by the fence, cross the boggy burn and climb up to a gate by an old sheepfold, which you passed on your outward walk.

9 Turn right over the stile and return to the parking area by following your outward route.

Curlew

Practicals

Type of walk: Very pleasing, with some exciting scrambling up to the trig point on Craig Obney. Enjoy all the magnificent views as you go.

Total distance:	8 miles/13km
Time:	4–5 hours
Map:	OS Landranger 52 or 53/Explorer 379
NB:	Do not attempt the ascent to Craig Obney in the mist or in the shooting season.

Birnam Hill

To park, leave the A9 at the A923 turn-off for Dunkeld. In a few yards turn right for Birnam and park in a large layby, grid ref 032418, on the right side of the road.

Birnam Hill. The steepish climb to the summit is rewarded by superb views over the Perthshire Highlands and southwards towards the fertile lowland plains. The hill is famed for its Shakespearean associations; it was here that King Duncan's son Malcolm is reputed to have made camp before marching to Dunsinane to defeat Macbeth.

The famous **Birnam Oak** is said to be the last relic of ancient Birnam Wood. The surrounding hills support fine woodland, much of it carefully planted during the last two centuries by the Dukes of Atholl and, more recently, by the Forestry Commission.

Birnam is the sister community of Dunkeld, with the two settlements linked by Telford's Bridge over the Tay. The seven-arched bridge was built in 1809, and its toll-house can still be seen. The village owes its existence largely to the 19th century railway builders who sited Dunkeld Station on the south bank of the Tay. It was built here, in 1856, because the 6th Duke of Atholl refused to let the railway cross his estates. It took another seven years for the Duke to agree to the railway

Stair bridge

continuing over his land on its way to Inverness. During this time English families rented villas in Birnam – among them was Beatrix Potter's family.

1 Walk past the public toilets on the opposite side of the road. Turn right and walk on along Birnam Glen, signposted Birnam Hill Walk. Pass under the A9 and the bridge carrying the Perth to Inverness railway. Use the footpath on the left to continue uphill. Look through the trees for the pretty waterfall on the Inchewan Burn. Follow the signpost for the Birnam Hill Walk and King's Seat, crossing a narrow road and walking uphill along a leafy track.

Walk 21

2 At a junction where there is a 'Private—No Entry' sign, bear right and then left, following the Inchewan Burn. Soon a waymark directs you left and steeply uphill through silver birch, oak and willow, with wood sage and bracken beneath. A strategically placed seat gives you a chance to get your breath. Continue climbing, with many a stop to look back at the pleasing views. Look for the Telford Bridge over the Tay, and then the three lochs north-east of Dunkeld. Soon the bracken is left behind and you move into heather, cowberry and bilberry.

3 Follow the clear path to climb onto a craggy viewpoint (1000ft/306m) and here you will want to linger. Stride on over the heather-clad crown where you might see red deer race between larches. Keep to the path

ahead, as you cross a wet patch and then, in the centre of a vast area of heather, rears a large mound. This is King's Seat (1333ft/404m) and from its summit the whole of Perthshire seems to lie at your feet.

4 A waymark directs you off the summit. Climb the next slope where a little scrambling is required. Now below you can see the A9 winding into the distance. Below too, stands picturesque Rohallion Lodge, with its conical turrets, sitting beside an artificial lake. Begin the steeply stepped descent, and follow the waymark at the bottom, which directs you right. Keep to the path and continue where it becomes a track. Alpine club moss grows about the way.

5 Stride the now-grassy track, which has more waymarks to keep you safely on the route. It swings left and begins to drop down and down into a birch glade. Turn right at the arrow and signboard for Stair Bridge, passing through birch and rowan. To the left, look for the battlemented start of the bridge. Descend the narrow path and cross a small stream, Birnam Burn, to see the splendid single-arched bridge high above you. Return from the stream to stand on the bridge and enjoy the fine views of woodland and several lochans. Retrace your steps to the signpost for Stair Bridge.

6 Continue on, passing a stone seat. Head along the path to take the well signposted left turn for Rohallion Castle, the remains of an old tower. Some effort has been made to reconstruct the building. It is in a hidden hollow with a good view over the countryside below.

7 Head back to the main path and carry on downhill. To visit King's Rock continue along the track, passing through a high gate. Ignore the right turn to Rohallion Lodge and stride along the easy-to-walk ride in the direction of Birnam Wood. This takes you to the grand viewpoint.

8 Walk back along the track to the high gate. Turn right to follow a narrow path that drops steadily through magnificent birch woodland

Alpine clubmoss

that masks Birnam Quarry. At the bottom of the long trail, turn right and walk to the gate before a railway bridge. Pass to the right of the gate and walk below the bridge.

9 Turn left to walk along the B867, Bankfoot Road. At the A9, cross, with care, and walk left in the direction of Inverness. In 59yds/46m turn right to take the old road leading into Birnam. After another 100yds/92m, look for the stile signposted Birnam circular walk. Stroll the metalled road and continue along the track beyond. Waymarks direct you to the riverside walk beside the fast-flowing River Tay. Walk this lovely path beneath enormous beeches and oaks. Continue past a children's park and then turn left just before the Birnam Oak. The track leads to the main street of Birnam. Turn right to regain your car.

Wood sage

Practicals

Type of walk: A steep hill walk taking you through mixed woodland, over heathery moorland, past a ruined castle, by a fascinating bridge and returning beside the River Tay.

Distance:	7 miles/11.4km
Time:	4 hours
Map:	OS Landranger 52/Explorer 379

22

River Ericht, Blairgowrie

Park in the Mill Inch free car park, grid ref 180453, which is signposted down a narrow lane on the north side of Wellmeadow Green at the centre of Blairgowrie.

Cargill's Leap. This is now seen from a viewing platform erected by the local council. From here you look down on the racing river, which is divided by huge boulders into two streams. The smaller stream flows through a narrow deep chasm that confines the roaring water. The main stream passes down an even narrower canyon and rages and foams in fury at its fetters. And then both streams unite to fall into a large deep pool where salmon leap. This part of the river

Cargill's Leap

is known as Cargill's Leap – named after a local man who in 1681 leapt across the narrow chasm to escape his pursuers.

Raspberries and Jute This part of Perthshire, with its sandstone loam, is the centre of the soft fruit industry that is restoring the prosperity first brought by the jute mills.

1 Walk northwards beside the fast-flowing River Ericht. Climb the steps that rise steeply on the left and turn right. Step out along the wide track through woodland high above the river. At the junction take the right fork, which leads back towards the river. Follow the path to reach the platform from which you can view Cargill's Leap. Return to the path and continue onwards. Look across the river to see a now-defunct jute mill that made use of the Ericht's water-power.

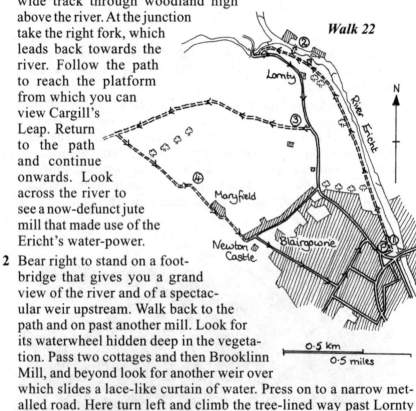

Walk 22

2 Bear right to stand on a foot-bridge that gives you a grand view of the river and of a spectacular weir upstream. Walk back to the path and on past another mill. Look for its waterwheel hidden deep in the vegetation. Pass two cottages and then Brooklinn Mill, and beyond look for another weir over which slides a lace-like curtain of water. Press on to a narrow metalled road. Here turn left and climb the tree-lined way past Lornty farm to the top.

3 Turn right into an un-made road and walk uphill, with acres of raspberries growing on either side. Carry on up and then 200yds/180m before the reinforced track turns sharp right, look for a kissing gate on the left almost hidden by vegetation. Beyond the gate follow the path which stretches ahead between two enormous fields. Look for tiny white pansies and red hemp nettle growing in the rough

grass edging the path. Pass through a kissing gate at its end and sit on the seat beyond. Enjoy the view, using the indicator set on a boulder, next to the seat, that describes the valley below and the hills beyond.

4 Follow the wide track that drops downhill. The way passes Maryfield farm under a row of lofty poplars, and on to Newton Road. Turn right to walk past Newton Castle. At the end of the road, turn left into Perth Street and follow it round until you reach the lane going down to the car park.

Pansies, trefoil, thyme

Practicals

Type of walk: This is a most enjoyable easy walk along a lovely river and returning through fields.

Total distance:	4 miles/6.4km
Time:	2½ hours
Map:	OS Landranger 53/Explorer 381

23

Den of Alyth and
the Hill of Alyth

Take the minor road which leaves Alyth Square on the south side
and continue past the church, on the right, and the Alyth Burn on
the left. This is the road to Bamff, and shortly after passing the de-
restriction sign the Den of Alyth car park is signposted on the left,
grid ref 235487.

Den. The Den, the deep-sided wooded valley of the Alyth Burn, is
designated a site of special scientific interest. The steep cliffs and the
bouldery bed of the Alyth burn were shaped by glaciers moving south
from the main Cairngorm ice mass. The valley has been wooded for

Path, Den of Alyth

several thousand years. The steep sides of the Den have probably protected the woods by making the removal of timber difficult.

Alyth is a farming town. Throughout the centuries it has managed to avoid destruction. It once earned its living by jute milling and weaving. Local layered and jointed sandstone, quarried nearby, was used to build Alyth as it expanded rapidly in the 1800s.

Walk 23

1 Start down the steps towards the picnic and children's play area, walking upstream. Stroll the path beneath alder, sycamore, oak, hazel and ash. Where the way branches, take the left fork, to continue below the huge Old Red Sandstone cliffs, shadowing the dancing Alyth Burn. The rock face is covered with lichens, mosses, ferns and small trees that precariously find a foothold. Walk on through a clearing and then beneath some magnificent beech to a footbridge, which you cross.

2 Follow the path to the right and climb the steep slope, the way littered with beech mast. The river flows far below to the right. Descend the slope and follow the path, which leads to an attractive stone bridge, built in 1914. Cross and turn left to continue along a path through trees, with the river to the left. Follow the path as it swings right and comes to a road.

3 Turn left to stride the shady road to a junction. Take the right branch, signposted Glenisla. Walk uphill, with a conifer plantation to the right. Beyond the woodland, in summer, the right side of this minor road is bordered with great clumps of gorse

and spiked with foxgloves. Carry on until you reach a signpost for the Hill of Alyth.

4 A path climbs right, up the gorse-covered slope, which is overrun by rabbits. Follow the path as it swings left then right to join a wider track. Climb steadily to the left, keeping an extensive bank of gorse to your left, as you make for the highest point ahead. Suddenly you come upon a delightful lochan nestling in the fold of the hill-top.

5 Once over the top of the hill, aim for a track (an old drove road) beside a wire fence that runs downhill to a clump of scots pines. Beneath these is a kissing gate, which gives access to a fenced track. Enjoy the gentle walk downhill. Pass through another kissing gate, turn left and then almost immediately right down another track.

Rabbit

6 When you have passed the farm-yard on your right, turn right into Strathmore Terrace and follow the road along which you drove earlier. The car park is a short distance along on the left.

Practicals

Type of walk: Delightfully easy walk of five miles passing through glorious woodland, beside a pleasing burn and over a hilltop with a splendid view.

Total distance:	5 miles/8km
Time:	3 hours
Maps:	OS Landranger 53/Explorer 381

24

Carn Gorm/Carn Mairg Horseshoe

Park at Invervar, grid ref 666483. To reach this look for a private track, signposted Inverinain and Dericambus, on the south side of the minor road from Fortingall to Bridge of Balgie. There is a parking area, on the right, a few yards down the track.

Ptarmigan are mountain grouse. They breed and live all year on the high tops. In winter their plumage is all white and provides perfect camouflage. In spring, after moulting, their bodies are grey with white feathered bellies and white under the wings. They feed on the shrubby heath vegetation found at high altitudes. When disturbed they scuttle away among the rocks, flying off only if in imminent danger. They live in families during the summer and congregrate in large parties over the winter. Listen for their hoarse cackles as they take off when disturbed. When they land they begin to call again making quiet motorbike noises.

Inverar. This was once a thriving village with a school, shop, tailor, carpenter, weaver and a lint mill. Today little remains; the old mill, a small round building with a conical roof, sits in an idyllic woodland hollow beside a glacial mound with a leat from the burn running downhill.

Ben Lawers and Beinn Ghlas from Carn Gorm

1 Return to the road, cross and go through the gate on the left of a stone building opposite. There are notices on the gate about access and stalking dates. Walk up the track past some cottages on the left. Cross left to see the remains of the lint mill. Follow the way as it crosses an open field, then winds up through a conifer wood. Emerge from the trees by a gate onto open fell. Continue on an excellent track, with the lovely Invervar Burn foaming below to your left.

2 Cross a side burn, the Allt Coire a' Chearcaill, on a stout bridge. Just before the next tributary joins the Invervar the deer fence, which has been beside you, turns away left and there is a footbridge over the Invervar Burn. Cross this and follow a good 'walkers' path along the riverbank to the end of the plantation. Here the path ascends the river terrace, scree covered and eroded. Aim for the small ruin above.

3 Beyond, go on the generally clear path leading up onto the spur of Carn Gorm, a shoulder below the summit, where the ground is stony. The summit (3370ft/1029m) has a cairn and is higher than the point to the north where the trig point lies on its side and is surrounded by a low wall. In mid-summer the schist is covered with clumps of moss campion and alpine ladies' mantle. The grass is spangled with mountain pansies.

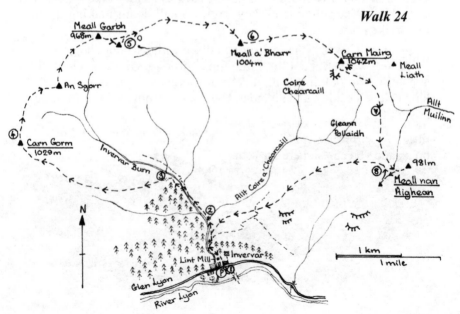

Walk 24

4 Take the obvious path that leads quite steeply down to the north, to a col below the small top of An Sgorr. There are two ancient fence posts and the base of a wall and the path follows this to the top of the hill. Descend north to the next col and then climb gently, north-east, towards Meall Garbh (3171ft/968m). At the shoulder half way up a line of old rusty fence posts appears, and these can be followed to the top. Meall Garbh has two rocky summits of similar height. The north-west one, situated on the fence line, is slightly higher and is adorned with a stone and fence post sculpture for a cairn.

5 Descend easily, north east to the next col, passing a small lochan, a likely place for spotting ptarmigan. Follow the fence over the col and east up the long gradual ascent towards Meall a' Bharr (3313ft/1004m). On reaching the ridge turn south-east and continue to the summit cairn on a small rocky outcrop.

6 Turn east again still keeping with the fence and continue along the ridge, descending slightly. The path then diverges from the fence and follows easier ground to the south. It then rises to the summit of Carn Mairg (3436ft/1042m) with its well built substantial cairn. Descend south east following a steepish path down through a boulder field. From the bottom of this a clear path contours round above the corrie of Gleann Pollaidh to the col between this and Gleann Muilinn where you might stumble on families of golden plovers.

7 Follow the path over the col and onto Meall nan Aighean (3213ft/981m) which becomes slightly indistinct higher up but the going is good. There are two summits and you arrive between them. The east one is the higher and consists of a pleasant little rocky tor. It is a good wind-break and you can sit here for your tea break and look over towards Schiehallion. A distinct path takes you along the top to the west summit with a superb view down onto Glen Lyon, with the river shining in the sunlight. Beyond lies the Lawers range, dark and imposing.

Ptarmigan

8 Return towards the col but before reaching it, drop down over grass, winding towards a path seen below. This heads off to the west down a long ridge and is a lovely way to descend. It is easily angled and mostly good underfoot, with fine views of the Lawers Hills and Glen Lyon. Towards the foot of the ridge a stalker's path crosses the walker's path. Continue on along the ridge on the walker's path and descend with it to join your outward route just above the point at which it leaves the wood. Retrace your steps from here to your car.

Practicals

Type of walk: This is a superb walk with magnificent views through a quiet unspoiled area. It is a big walk though generally easy and straight forward. In mist the fence along the top is a good guide, but it is foolish to go up in uncertain weather without some prior experience of navigation. The ridges are big and not always well defined and a walker, in bad weather, could end up in quite the wrong place. On a long summer's day you will want to go on and on over the tops.

Total distance:	10–11 miles/16–17km
Time:	7 hours
Map:	OS Landranger 51/Explorer 378

NB The former strongly deterrrent notice on the gate has been replaced by more emollient ones which thank hill-walkers for their co-operation and define the deer-stalking season to be avoided. This is primarily from September to 21st October, but continues intermittently until the following mid-February. Notices are posted on the gate to announce days to avoid. To check in advance, phone 01887 877267 during office hours, or contact the head stalker in early evening on 01887 830312. You can also visit the estate website at www.chesthill.com.

You are still exhorted to keep to the clockwise ridge circuit described here, and discouraged from taking dogs, which must be kept on a lead at the very least.

25

Schiehallion

Park in the large car park at Braes of Foss, just off narrow Schiehallion road, which runs between Kinloch Rannoch and Loch Kinnardochy, grid ref 753557.

Schiehallion means 'The fairy place of the Caledonians'. At 3553ft/1083m, it is considered Scotland's most perfect mountain due to its symmetrical cone shape; it is what everyone thinks a mountain should look like. In 1774 an expedition led by the Reverend Nevil Maskelyne, the Astronomer Royal, found its shape ideal for experiments to find the weight of the earth. One of the members of the

*Schiehallion from
River Tummel*

expedition was a Charles Hutton, who first thought of using contour lines, now universally used on today's maps.

John Muir (1838–1914) was a conservationist and a visionary and one of the first persons to call for the conservation of wild places for their own sake. The John Muir Trust was founded in Scotland in 1983, to conserve the remaining wild places for people and for nature. The Trust owns nearly 45,000 acres in the Scottish highlands and islands. In 1999 East Schiehallion was bought by the Trust and they began replacing the old boggy badly eroded track, used when this book was first published in 1992, with a properly constructed path that zigzags up the slopes to a flattish area.

Walk 25

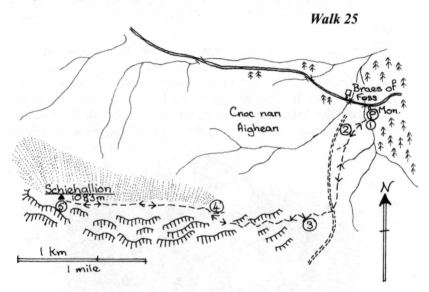

1 Walk to the end of the parking area and follow the narrow path to a gate. Beyond, cross a bridge over a small stream bordered with bog myrtle. Follow the clear, easy-to-walk path over pasture where, in summer, it is colourful with wild flowers. To the left lies a large stand of conifers.

2 Stride out into moorland, which in late summer is a pink haze with heather. After ¼ mile/0.5km ignore the cart track that bisects the path and continue on aiming for the mountain ahead.

3 The "new" path then begins to zigzag upwards, making use of several rocky steps, to around 2860ft/870m, where the path stops.

4 Continue on up the ridge over scattered boulders, heading for a large cairn. Pick your way carefully on an indistinct path through ankle wrenching rubble towards what appears to be the summit when, over the brow, there is another to surmount. This goes on several times until you reach a series of large boulders of quartz. It is exhilarating to step from boulder to boulder, gradually nearing the top, but requires considerable concentration and nimbleness, though the boulders do lead fairly quickly to the summit. The great reward though, when you do attain the top, is the magnificent view of Perthshire's other peaks and more.

5 To return, it is best to retrace your outward route; there really is no other safe way. Do take care over the quartzite boulders.

Cloudberry

Practicals

Type of walk: This is a very good climb but walking boots, waterproofs, a map and compass are essential and care should be taken when stepping from boulder to boulder. Do not attempt in the mist.

Total distance: 6½ miles/10km there and back (2,500ft/750m of ascent)

Time: 4–5 hours

26

Kinloch Rannoch and Craig Varr

Park in the riverside car park on the B846, ½ mile/0.8km east of Kinloch Rannoch, grid ref 669587.

Loch Rannoch is magnificent: a long, narrow, deep ribbon of water, hemmed in by steep hillsides. At the western end lies the lonely Rannoch Moor, an empty wilderness traversed by a railway line uniquely engineered to "float" on the unstable mosses which it crosses.

Scots Pine This beautiful native tree, slower to grow than many plantation imports, but much hardier, was once the dominant species in the vast Caledonian Forest, of which only small areas remain standing. One such is the Black Wood of Rannoch on the south side of the loch, well worth a visit after the walk. The upper ridge of Craig Varr supports a few rather pathetic specimens, some bent double by the relentless westerlies.

1 Cross the road at the east end of the car park and go through a high steel gate to follow a gradually rising path, with a fence and mixed woodland on the right. A burn is crossed, above a small, dense conifer plantation down on the right. Just before reaching a big pylon, take a track branching off left up the hill toward another plantation. The track

Falls of Allt Mor, Kinloch Rannoch

passes close to these trees, on their right. On reaching the corner of the wood, look left for the line of a dilapidated wall.

2 Cross the wall and pick up the indistinct path coming up from the valley which makes its way, left, up the hillside parallel to the broken wall. When the wall levels out, then turns away down the slope to the left, the path keeps going onwards and upwards, making straight for the lee of the steep eastern flank of Ceann Caol na Creige, the first objective of this walk. The path disappears from time to time on boggy ground, but press on keeping close to the steep slope on the left until a col is reached, marked by a small cairn set on a flat rock, up on its left.

3 Here turn up the slope, leaving the col to scale the pathless and heather-clad north ridge of Ceann Caol na Creige. The summit has a substantial cairn from which, on a clear day, most of Loch Rannoch, Kinloch Rannoch village and Schiehallion are well displayed. Behind looms the bulk of Beinn a'Chuallaich.

4 From the highest point of the walk, drop down a narrow path ahead which soon leads to the first of the beautifully cone-shaped cairns gracing the summit ridge of Craig Varr. Look around at the ever-widening view and count the cairns as you descend towards the scattering of wind-battered Scots Pine which adorn the brow of Craig Varr's precipice.

5 When the fifth cairn is reached (just beyond a group of trees bent double) you have a fine full-length view of Loch Rannoch with the mountains above Glencoe and Rannoch Moor an impressive backdrop behind it. Your path down the mountainside starts from here, and leads you across the moor below to a recently constructed track (not marked on the OS maps), by a gate.

6 Do not go through the gate, but turn right up the track, over a shoulder of the hill and down to a bridge over the Allt Mor, which tumbles in a series of delightful

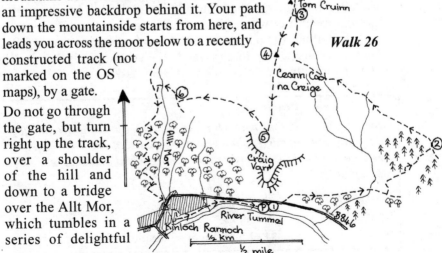

Walk 26

95

falls towards the village. By the bridge stands a conical Craig Varr cairn, guiding ascending walkers to the path you have just followed, and re-assuring you that this is the way down. Go left after the bridge, join the droving track coming down from the right and reach another gate, with a stile. This you do cross, going down the steadily-graded s-bends with the Allt Mor falling noisily down on your left. Greenfinches and other woodland birds can be seen and heard as you head down through the trees to Kinloch Rannoch village. If by this time you are hoping for a nice cup of tea, go across the road for a short distance opposite Brown's Garage to the Post Taste tearoom, which, not surprisingly, occupies part of the post office building. Then go back and turn down Allt-mor Crescent, opposite the track you recently descended, bearing right beyond the chapel and following the sign for Riverside

Scots Pine and cone cairn

Walk. Go left to cross the footbridge over the Allt Mor to continue through trees and, where the track swings left toward the houses, go ahead along the narrow riverside path. The fast flowing River Tummel is an exciting foreground to the view towards Schiehallion. In a few minutes you are back in the car park.

Practicals

Type of walk: A famous rocky bluff is climbed by a little-frequented but mainly easy-graded route, with the reward of great views from the ridge, and a descent through charming woodland beside a rushing burn.

Total distance:	4½ miles/7.2km
Time:	3 hours
Maps:	OS Landranger 42/Explorer 386

27

Allean Forest and Loch Bhac

Park in the Queen's View Centre by Loch Tummel, grid ref 864598.

Queen's View. Before you start the walk, visit the viewpoint from which Queen Victoria viewed Loch Tummel and Schiehallion, the well-shaped mountain at the head of the loch. Though the weather was fine for her and the view good, the Queen records in her diary not her thoughts about the view but about the poor cup of tea brewed on her picnic. We can all appreciate her feelings.

Loch Bhac

The **Clachan** is a typical 18th-century farm settlement, parts of which have been reconstructed. Notice the cornkiln on the right, later used as a limekiln. Beyond stands a ruin that was possibly a milking byre. On the left of the track lies a house and an animal house. Both have been restored and have splendid turf roofs.

1   Leave the visitor centre and walk up the road to the left for a few steps. When you reach the road sign telling drivers coming from the west that they will reach the visitor centre in 100yds/92m, take a faint path that leads up the slope on the right. After a dozen steps the path becomes

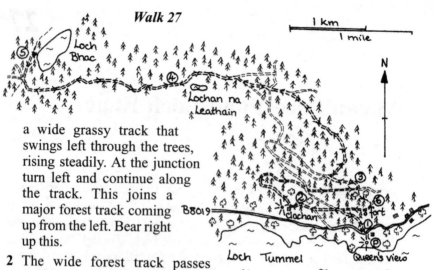

Walk 27

a wide grassy track that swings left through the trees, rising steadily. At the junction turn left and continue along the track. This joins a major forest track coming up from the left. Bear right up this.

2 The wide forest track passes through mixed woodland to the 'clachan'. Follow the sign for a good viewpoint to see Schiehallion and Loch Tummel. Return to the track and continue upwards; the way in summer is lined with flowers. Follow the frequent waymarks. At a cross of tracks, continue ahead for half a mile and then wind round left. After less than half a mile, turn sharp right ascending another forestry track and leaving the waymarks behind.

3 Remain on the main track uphill, eventually to enjoy a magnificent view across open countryside to Beinn A'Ghlo. Walk on through more acres of conifers and then a clear-felled hillside opens up wide, glorious views of the mountains opposite. Carry on along the track until you reach Lochan na Leathain. Pause here and enjoy the reed-fringed pool. Beyond the lochan the track comes close to extensive heather moorland. Schiehallion now seems very close.

4 After this pleasing open part of the track you move back into the forest. Go quietly and you might see red deer or a capercaillie. After a gradual descent, a signpost is reached which directs those coming from the opposite direction to their left, and your right, for Loch Bhac. There are two tracks with 'public footpath' signs. Take the right-hand one, past a padlocked gate for the short, tree-lined track to the loch. The first view of this lovely sheet of water, with its small boats, makes the long trek through the forest worth while. At the head of the loch lies the magnificent Beinn A'Ghlo. Here the silence is broken only by the sound of an occasional fish jumping for flies. This is the place for your picnic.

5 To return, retrace your steps, enjoying the dramatic views of the Perthshire hills, which appear ahead of you. When you reach the corner at point 3 on the map above, follow the waymarks directing you left into the trees along a grassy track. Very soon the way narrows and the route drops through deciduous woodland and, in summer, six-foot-high bracken.

6 On reaching a forest track, turn right and look for the signpost directing you left to a clearing in the forest and the site of a ninth century Pictish ring fort. Return to the track for a short distance and then turn sharp left when you reach a fire hydrant on the left, just before the next waymarked post. This is the track taken at the outset and it leads you easily back to the visitor centre.

Capercaillie (displaying)

Practicals

Type of walk: This is a long walk, generally easy underfoot. It takes you through forestry to lovely Loch Bhac, with grand views along the way.

Total distance:	10½ miles/17km
Time:	5–6 hours
Map:	OS Landranger 43/Explorer 386

28

Linear Walk from Pitlochry to Grandtully, visiting the Dunfallandy Stone and Clachan an Diridh

NB This is an excellent two-car cross country trek. The best way is to leave one car at the end of the walk and drive with all your party, and their walking gear, to the beginning, then afterwards drive together back to Pitlochry to retrieve the other car. An alternative is to try to time your walk to enable you to catch one of the infrequent buses that run from Grandtully to Pitlochry. It is essential to check bus times at Pitlochry before setting out to do this; the bus runs only on certain days.

Standing stones

Park one car in the car park at the old station yard, behind the Grandtully Hotel, grid ref 913531 and the other beyond the entrance to the Dunfallandy House Hotel, grid ref 946567.

Dunfallandy Stone. This Pictish cross slab, probably carved in about the ninth century, records the conversion of the area's inhabitants to Christianity. On the front is a cross divided into panels of interlaced ornament and flanked by angels and beasts. On the back, framed by two serpents, are figures seated on either side of a cross, a horseman, tools and five of the enigmatic Pictish symbols. The monument is cared for by Historic Scotland. It is set behind glass, protected and preserved for all to enjoy.

Clachan an Diridh. In a quiet atmospheric clearing among Scots Pine, to the right of the route, a narrow path leads to several standing stones.

1 Walk on for 100yds/91m to an ancient monument sign on the right. A narrow road leads to a flight of steps that climb to the Dunfallandy Stone. Return to where

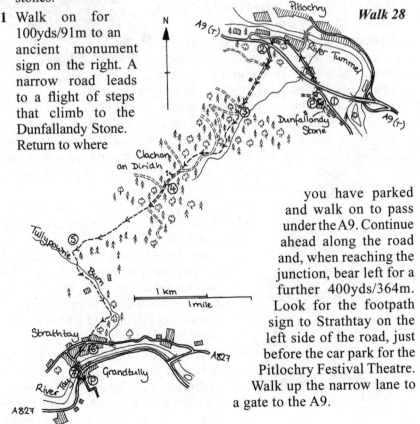

you have parked and walk on to pass under the A9. Continue ahead along the road and, when reaching the junction, bear left for a further 400yds/364m. Look for the footpath sign to Strathtay on the left side of the road, just before the car park for the Pitlochry Festival Theatre. Walk up the narrow lane to a gate to the A9.

2 Cross the main road with care, and press on along the lane, passing farm buildings. Head uphill through pastures. Carry on up the reinforced forestry track. Pass a huge rock to the left of the track. Look for the clearly signposted left turn, a grassy path that leads into the forest.

3 The path climbs steadily through mixed woodland. Away to the left a tiny stream gurgles and chatters merrily. On reaching a forest road look left to see extensive heather-covered moorland. Cross the road and pick up the well signposted grassy path that leads into the forest once more, where you might see dozens of Scotch Argus and fritillary butterflies flitting about the ride. This path soon rejoins the forest road; follow the signpost direction arm straight ahead from the junction. Look for a clearing on the right. A narrow path leads to the standing stones, set among pines.

4 Continue along the track and walk to a ladder stile, which gives access to open moorland where sheep graze. A narrow path leads diagonally right with white-topped

Scotch Argus

posts to guide you on your way. Ahead are glorious views of the Tay valley, with Aberfeldy to the right and Schiehallion to the far right. Pass through a gate and continue dropping gently downhill, with heather-covered slopes, forested hills and mountains tops stretching ahead of you.

Juniper

5 Pass through large clumps of juniper to a gate in the deer fence. Turn left as directed to walk beside the fence. From now on the way drops rapidly, before and after crossing the Tullypowrie Burn. The path keeps to the right bank of the burn for some time, then swings off to the right through the golf course to reach Strathtay.

6 When you reach the road, turn right and then fork left. At the end of this short road, turn left and cross the narrow road bridge over the River Tay. On your right are the rapids which have become famous as a course for white-water canoeists. If you arrive when an event is taking place, the whole area will be crowded with excited competitors and spectators.

7 On the far side of the bridge you are in Grandtully. Turn right and make for the car park, a short distance up on the left, to retrieve your second vehicle.

Small pearl-bordered fritillary

Practicals

Type of walk: This is a very satisfactory hill walk along good paths through farmland, moorland and coniferous woodland. Enjoy the fine views of the Tummel and Tay valleys.

Distance:	6 miles/9.8km
Time:	2½ hours. Add on driving time at each end.
Maps:	OS Landranger 52/Explorer 386

29

Black Spout and Edradour, Pitlochry

Park in the car park, grid ref 950576, for the start of the walk to Black Spout and Edradour. It is well signposted and lies to the south east of Pitlochry on the north side of the A924.

Black Spout. A web of foot-paths leads from Pitlochry to the lovely waterfall on the Edradour Burn. Black Spout, 195ft/60m descends first in white-topped cascades and then plummets in a very long foaming drop into a dark pool. Finally, the surging white water falls for a third time before racing on downhill. The amphitheatre, over which descends spectacular twin falls, is lined with rowan, birch, hazel, oak, elm and ivy. Black Spout is a sight not to be missed.

Edradour, claimed to be the smallest and one of the most pic-turesque distilleries in Scotland, uses the clear waters of the burn. This originates from deep on Moulin Moor and bubbles through peat and granite before surfacing a few hundred paces

Black Spout

away from the distillery. Local barley is malted and dried over peat fires. Edradour was established in 1825.

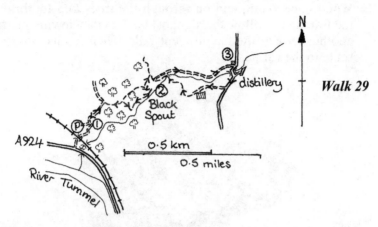

Walk 29

1 From the car park follow the signpost directions for the woodland walk. Head up the wide reinforced track and where it branches take the right fork through oak woodland. Turn right and follow the signpost for Black Spout, and walk uphill through the oaks to a splendid viewing platform *Goldenrod* This was provided by the Rotary Club of Pitlochry and constructed by Aberdeen University Officer Training Corps in July 1989.

2 When you can drag yourself away from the dramatic fall, follow the signpost for Edradour, continuing through oak woodland where wood sage, harebell, devil's bit scabious and golden rod flower in late summer. When the path divides for Moulin and Edradour, fork right following the waymarks and go up to a wall. Here bear left, keeping the wall on your right, with the burn falling noisily, but hidden by lush vegetation. On your left is a fenced field which usually has a crop of barley, and beyond, a fine view of Ben Vrackie. (After visiting the waterfall you may wish to visit the distillery.)

3 To continue the walk, leave the path, turn right to carry on for 50yds/46m along the narrow road in front of the distillery and turn right again to an access road that leads to Colivoulin farm.

105

Continue past the dwelling and follow the waymark through a gate and along a path. This leads to a kissing gate into Black Spout Wood once again, and on through the trees to a footbridge over the Edradour. Follow the signpost back to the viewing platform for another look at the magnificent falls. Then retrace your outward route to the car park.

Primroses, wood sorrel and golden saxifrage

Practicals

Type of walk: A short walk through mainly oak woodland and pastures to a spectacular waterfall and on to view, or visit, a distillery.

Total distance:	2 miles/3.4km
Time:	1–2 hours
Maps:	OS Landranger 52/Explorer 386

30

The Pass of Killiecrankie and the Linn of Tummel

Park in the Killiecrankie Visitor Centre car park, grid ref 917627.

Soldier's Leap. From a walled area on the walk you can overlook the Soldier's Leap, where the River Garry races through a deep gorge. In 1689 the Government army, led by General McKay, was ambushed and defeated by the pursuing Highlanders. Here one of the fleeing Redcoat Lowlanders leaped 18½ ft/6m over the raging burn and escaped the Jacobites. You also pass the Balfour Stone, reputed to be the grave of Brigadier Barthold Balfour. He was part of the General's army and he died as he tried to escape.

The Falls of Tummel. A visit by Queen Victoria to see these magnificent falls was commemorated by a small monument, which still stands on a rocky promontory. Alas, since the creation of the hydro-electric scheme, completed in 1950, the height and volume of the falls has been reduced. To avoid disappointment to visitors the tempestuous stretch of water

River Garry, Killiecrankie

has been renamed the Linn of Tummel. Look for the old fish pass, which enabled salmon to avoid the falls on their journey upstream. In 1944 the Linn of Tummel, with 50 acres of woodland, was presented to the National Trust by Dr G.F. Barbour.

1 From the car park, follow the signpost directions for the Soldier's Leap and the Linn of Tummel, using the National Trust for Scotland's foot-path. Walk past the Trooper's Den. Here a soldier drew first blood for the Jacobites by shooting a cavalry officer, before the Battle of Killiecrankie. Walk ahead to sit on a seat to enjoy the grand view of the Garry River.

2 Continue on through the birch and oak woodland. Bear right to follow the signpost to the walled area overlooking the Soldier's Leap. Then return to the signpost and continue through the pass, along the densely tree-lined path. Walk below the 510ft/155m long viaduct, which was designed for the Inverness and Perth Junction Railway by Joseph Mitchell and completed in 1863 at a cost of £5,730. The 10 masonry arches were faced with bricks, which saved the cost of dressed stone used for the pillars.

3 Stride on along the path high above the Garry and past the Balfour Stone. Continue through a hazel copse and turn right to follow the Linn of Tummel trail. Walk onto the Garry Bridge and look down on the steep gorge below. The water is deep and dark, with lush vegeta-tion lining its banks. Glorious beech trees clothe slopes above.

4 Cross the bridge and turn left to follow the signs for the Linn. Walk downhill with the river to the left. Beyond, open pastures stretch away to the right. Continue beneath beeches and then climb a flight

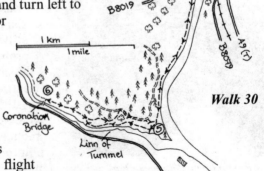

Walk 30

of steps. At the branching of paths, take the lower one. At the signpost for the Coronation Bridge, turn left and walk down to the monument commemorating Queen Victoria's visit.

5 Walk back to the path and carry on along a fenced area from where there is a dramatic view of the raging water, imprisoned in its narrow gorge. Then follow a lovely stretch of the plunging river, the path passing beneath Scots Pine and heather. Stroll on along the path as it moves away from the river through an open area and then on into mixed woodland. Follow the signpost for the Coronation Bridge, a long metal suspension bridge from where there is a pleasing view of the lively burn. Do **not** cross.

6 Return to the open area and walk back to the signpost for the bridge. Here follow the waymark pointing uphill to pass through a large planting of Douglas Fir. Walk the airy forest path high above the river, which is well waymarked. Ignore the right branch and continue. Stride on to a waymark pointing acute right. Follow the steps down to a fenced track. Turn right and drop down more steps to cross a narrow stream. Then climb steps and walk along the other side of open pasture, with deciduous woodland to the left. Pass through oaks to join the path taken on your outward journey. Retrace your outward route across the river and back up the track to the Visitor Centre.

Salmon

Practicals

Type of walk: This is a lovely walk beside a dramatic river and through magnificent woodland. All is peaceful now, with only a faint lingering atmosphere of the 17th century bloody battle that occurred here.

Total distance:	5 miles/8km
Time:	2½ hours
Maps:	OS Landrangers 43 and 52/Explorer 386

31

Ben Vrackie

From Pitlochry, take the A924 to Moulin. Turn left along Baledmund Road beyond the Moulin Inn and follow the signposted directions for the walk. The car park is situated among trees, grid ref 944597.

Ben Vrackie at 2757ft/841m high is not a Munro but it looks like one and feels like one as you ascend its steep slope to the summit. From here you might spot Ben Lawers, Schiehallion, Arthurs Seat in Edinburgh and the Cairngorms.

Ben Vrachie

1 Leave the car park by the well signposted path, keeping close to a small burn. Cross the burn on a track bridge and continue up the other side of the burn, inside the edge of the wood. On reaching a track, turn left. After 50 metres go right onto the path again. Then cross the footbridge and stride on to cross a second. Go through the kissing gate beside the deer gate onto open moor.

2 Follow the signpost and walk on, with a dramatic view of Ben Vrackie ahead. Continue over the moor to a seat. Sit here and, in summer, enjoy the colourful variety of wild flowers. Press ahead to a little burn, which is crossed where the path divides. Ignore a left

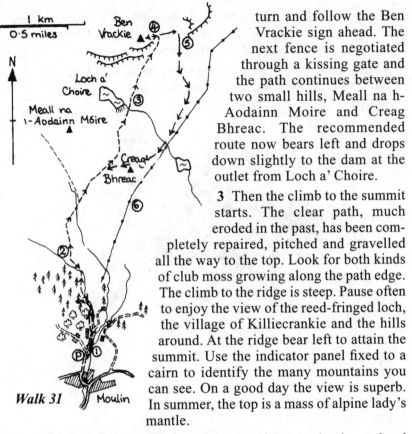

1 km
0.5 miles

N

Ben
Vrackie ④

⑤

Loch a'
Choire

③

Meall na
1-Aodainn Móire ▲

Creag
Bhreac
▲

⑥

②

P ①

Walk 31   Moulin

turn and follow the Ben Vrackie sign ahead. The next fence is negotiated through a kissing gate and the path continues between two small hills, Meall na h-Aodainn Moire and Creag Bhreac. The recommended route now bears left and drops down slightly to the dam at the outlet from Loch a' Choire.

3 Then the climb to the summit starts. The clear path, much eroded in the past, has been completely repaired, pitched and gravelled all the way to the top. Look for both kinds of club moss growing along the path edge. The climb to the ridge is steep. Pause often to enjoy the view of the reed-fringed loch, the village of Killiecrankie and the hills around. At the ridge bear left to attain the summit. Use the indicator panel fixed to a cairn to identify the many mountains you can see. On a good day the view is superb. In summer, the top is a mass of alpine lady's mantle.

4 Most people return by the same route. But if the weather is good and the moorland is an inviting sea of pink heather, you may be tempted to return from the secondary summit. If so, leave Ben Vrackie by a path leading north-east to the lower summit.

5 Then begin to drop downhill through heather in the direction of an unnamed loch to the left, south-east, of Loch a' Choire. Aim for the long wall that runs above the unnamed loch and to the left (south east) of Creag Bhreac. Keep to the right of the wall following a clear ATV (all-terrain vehicle) track downhill. Follow this

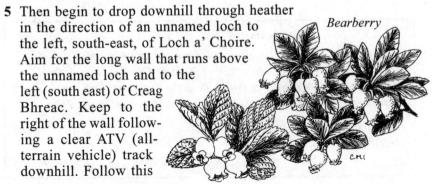

Bearberry

across the burn between the lochans and also where it curves up to rejoin the outward path at the top of the bealach between Creag Bhreac and Meall na h'Aodainn Moire.

6 Turn left and follow the path across the moorland to the kissing gate and then onwards along the well signed path to the car park.

Alpine lady's mantle

Practicals

Type of walk: This challenging walk crosses open moorland and then on up a steep hill path to the summit of Ben Vrackie, with spectacular views awaiting you. Choose a good day for your walk, wear boots, take waterproofs and a map. Do not attempt in the mist.

Total distance:	6½ miles/10.5km
Time:	4–5 hours
Maps:	OS Landranger 43 and 52/Explorer 386

32

Loch Errochty

Leave the A9 at Calvine and drive along the B847 through Struan to Trinafour. Cross the bridge over Errochty Water and continue up the slope past Trinafour House, which once was an inn. Beyond, on the right, lies the gate to a plantation of conifers. Park in the wide area by the gate, grid ref 725644, making sure not to obstruct the way for the farmer or forester.

Heathers I. Cross-leaved heath is widely distributed on high moorlands. It has large, pale-rose coloured, drooping flowers with pale almost to white on their under-sides. The leaves are arranged around the stem in whorls of four. **II.** Heather or Ling is found on moorlands all over Britain. The much branched stems are tough and wiry and the flowers pale pink or white. The flowers are persistent preserving much of their original form nine or ten months after they have opened. **III.** Purple heath has slender reddish-purple flowers and smooth stems and leaves. The latter are arranged in whorls around the stems in threes. This is the most characteristic plant of the moorland in early autumn, tracts of many acres being continuously covered by it.

Bridge, Loch Errochty

1 Pass through the gate and walk up the forest ride, which in summer is bordered with white fox-gloves and lined with larch. The way then passes through beech and on through conifers, climbing steadily, its banks lined with great clumps of heather. Be alert for your first glimpse of the huge dam that holds back Loch Errochty. Away to the left, beyond the treeline, the heather stretches upwards but not quite to the tops of the outliers of Beinn a' Chuallaich.

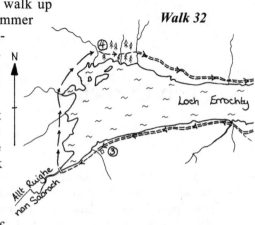

Walk 32

2 Once beyond the dam, the loch stretches ahead blue and sparkling. Here you might see black grouse fly up from feeding on the heather; they settle rapidly and are quickly lost to sight. Just before you cross a wooden footbridge look left to see a pretty burn, lined with heather and willow, tumbling in white-topped falls. Climb the tall stile to the right of the deer gate to pass out of the trees and onto open moorland. Stride the track as it keeps well above the loch, then follow it as it drops gently to come beside the silvery water. Look for the roots of great trees exposed along the water's edge if the level of the reservoir has dropped.

3 Follow the track as it passes a derelict cottage and walk on to a wooden footbridge over Allt Ruighe nan Saorach. It was built by Royal Navy Engineers in 1965, and has been repaired since the last edition of this book was published. Now you must make a decision. You can turn back and follow the pleasing track just walked. Or, cross the bridge and find your own way around the several inlets at the head of the loch – if there has been heavy rain the feeder burns may require wading or boulder hopping.

4 Aim for a large walled sheep pen on the north-western tip of the loch beyond the last inlet. From here there is a good path through the heather, which passes through a gate in the recently constructed deer fence and an enclave of conifers. Beyond this it becomes an easy-to-walk vehicle track running the length of the north side of the loch. Look back often for marvellous views of the western mountains with Ben Nevis towering over all.

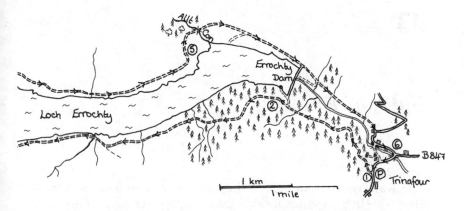

5 Soon the dam comes into view. Negotiate the platform kissing gate by the bridge over the Allt Con, and head along the track to pass the huge dam. Join the access road and continue onwards, looking right for a good view of Schiehallion. The track drops downwards to a gate. Beyond stride downhill, with Wade Bridge (now unsafe) to your right. Pass Bridge Cottage and continue to the junction.

6 Turn right to walk back to your car.

Black Grouse (lekking)

Practicals

Type of walk: This is a grand walk for when the acres of heather are in bloom – but watch out for the bees. To complete the circuit, choose a time during a dry spell, wear walking boots and be prepared for rougher and wetter walking around the head of the loch.

Total distance:	9 miles/14.5km
Time:	5 hours
Maps:	OS Landranger 42/Explorer 386

33

Falls of Bruar

The walk starts from behind the country shopping development House of Bruar. Approach either from a signposted turn off the main A9, or along the old road (now B8079) from Blair Atholl. Walkers are directed to use the House of Bruar car park, grid ref 822660. From this you can visit the adjacent Clan Donachaidh Museum, devoted to the history of the Robertsons, a powerful clan in these parts in their day.

Visitors

These lovely falls, considered the greatest in Perthshire, have attracted visitors for over 200 years, including Queen Victoria, William Wordsworth, Robert Burns and J.M.W. Turner. The burn tumbled through bare open hillside until the fourth Duke of Atholl began to plant the banks with trees in response to Burns' poem, 'Humble Petition of the Bruar Water'.

Falls of Bruar (upper fall)

View House. A stone arch is all that remains of the view-house. It was designed to obscure the view of the magnificent middle falls until the last moment, when you emerged from its walls.

Walk 33

0.5 km
0.5 miles

1 Leave the car park by an exit behind the restaurant and join a track signposted for the Bruar Falls. Pass through a tunnel beneath the Perth to Inverness railway. Beyond, a notice warns the public to beware of the dangerous cliffs. The path continues through very tall conifers. Notice the rock formations over which the river falls. Continue past a natural rock arch above which drop the lower falls. The lower bridge crosses above.

2 Walk to the stone arch to the left of the bridge. Head on uphill, remaining on the western side, passing through dense conifers, festooned with lichens. Large clumps of rhododendron thrive. Beside them grow hard fern with large fertile fronds, standing tall above the infertile ones. Continue on up the wide path until you come to the three arched upper bridge. Cross and press on upstream to the seats by a picnic site, from where there is a good view of the wooded ravine.

3 Return downstream, now on the east bank, and continue to a seat strategically placed for a dramatic view of the upper falls. Four small

Hard fern

117

cascades are followed by a spectacular fall, descending into a deep basin. Just above the pool the raging water creates a flickering rainbow.

4 Pass through the deer gate and follow the notice to another view point and the site of another old view-house. Go on down through the trees to cross the lower bridge and retrace your outward route to regain the car park.

Polypody

Grey Wagtail

Practicals

Type of walk: A short but steepish climb and descent, on good paths, beside a spectacular waterfall – a walk that is a must for all.

Total distance:	1 mile/1.6km
Time:	1½ hours
Maps:	OS Landranger 43/Explorer 386

Glen Tilt

Park in the parking area near the station at Blair Atholl, grid ref 870654.

Please note: On some weekdays in the spring and summer there is target shooting on the rifle range, during which the public are excluded from part of the route described below. To save a considerable diversion, check with the Atholl Estate Information Centre (01796 481646) before setting out, or look on the notice board in the castle car park.

Blair Castle. The castle, for many centuries the chief stronghold of the Earls and Dukes of Atholl, has by its strategic position in the central Highlands, witnessed many stirring events. The oldest part dates back to the time of the Crusader Earl David, who died in 1270. Edward III lodged at the castle in 1336. Mary Queen of Scots was entertained to a 'hunt' in the Atholl Forest in 1564. Between 1652 and

Gows Bridge

1660 the castle was occupied by a Cromwellian garrison. Prince Charles Stuart stayed at Blair twice and when the castle was occupied by a Hanoverian garrison the Prince's able lieutenant, General Lord George Murray, laid siege to his old home.

Gows Bridge is the furthest point of the Glen Tilt trail. If after crossing it, you continue upstream, climbing well above the river, the view unfolds of the U-shaped, glacially gouged trough of Glen Tilt. This was the old route through to upper Deeside and through the Lairig Ghru to Speyside and also used as a drove road by cattle drovers taking black cattle to market. They were driven over the hill to Glen Fernate and so to Kirkmichael, an important gathering point.

Walk 34

1 Walk past the Atholl Arms Hotel and the entrance to the Castle. Continue into the caravan site, which lies on the left. Turn right to take a gate leading to steps to the riverside path. Ahead lies the lovely River Tilt, gracious, wide, surging, brown with peat, and white-topped where it hastens round boulders. This is the start of the Glen Tilt Trail, which is marked with stage posts roughly one mile apart.

2 Head upstream along a good path beneath beech. Down to your right look for the York Cascade, where it makes a spectacular leap to join the Tilt. The cascade was named after a member of the Atholl family who

120

was appointed Archbishop of York. Walk ahead for an even better view of the waterfall and continue upwards. Carry on across a packhorse bridge to cross over a road and climb into mixed woodland with the Tilt far below to the right.

3 At the reinforced forest track, turn right (Stage one). Follow the arrow pointing right and walk along a narrow path, criss-crossed with tree roots. It makes a semi-circle through conifers and returns to the forest track. Turn right and walk on, with open pastures to the left and the home farm high above the fields (Stage 2). Leave the track by a waymark to the left and walk through deciduous woodland. This leads to an area of tall larch called Blairuachdar (meaning Upper Blair) wood (Stage 3). Head along the path and turn right on reaching another track.

4 Pass through a gate and read the instructions on the board before you progress close to the rifle-range. Follow the track as it drops downhill, ignoring various branches going off to the left towards the shooting butts, with the slopes of Meall Dail Min towering to the right. In summer the way is bordered with flowers, including the lovely field felwort. Below, the River Tilt races through a narrows in the gorge.

5 Where you reach the river again, cross a bridge over a tributary burn to come to a high ladder stile, over the deer fence on your left, which you climb (Stage 4). Ascend the forestry road to the top of a rise, where an arrow directs you off right into trees and along a path which passes the ruins of a settlement known as Ach Mhaire Bhig. Soon you emerge from the forest, and the path continues, marked by helpful arrows, across open ground some way above the river, and past more ruined cottages.

6 At Stage 5, walk on to a small bridge over the lovely Allt Mhairc. Perhaps this is the place you will choose for your picnic. Then climb the slope and bear left along a path in the bracken to a waymarked post on the edge of another ruined settlement built round a kiln. The kiln was probably used originally for drying corn and then for producing quicklime. Go on to cross a small tributary stream and continue to Gows Bridge, named after a man who kept a public house when many more people dwelt here.

7 Cross the bridge and turn right to walk past Marble Lodge (Stage 6), which takes its name from an outcrop of green marble found above the bridge. Continue along the road. Take the waymarked green track, an old right of way that runs above the estate road, soon to return to it. Look for lint pools close to the waymarked post. In these

shallow water-filled basins flax, grown in the glen, was soaked to make it easier to work.

8 Leave the estate road on a grassy track indicated by an arrow. Look right to see the truncated spurs of the very steep hills opposite and the extensive conifer planting. Continue along the grassy track, which seems to go, pleasingly, on and on. Walk on past Stage 8. Climb a stile by a metal gate and stroll through the trees of a natural birch wood. After a few minutes, a track forks off to the right. Follow this and begin the gradual descent through conifers. Take a right fork when the path branches and go on along a grassy path. It runs high above the Tilt gorge.

9 Pass through a gateway and cross a bridge over a rushing burn, where you might see a stoat dash across in front of you. Follow the track across an open area to a gate to the road. Turn right and walk downhill for 100yds/92m and then, opposite a modern house, turn right into woodland. Walk beneath an avenue of beech, steadily descending to Blair Atholl, keeping beside the lovely Tilt for the last part of the walk.

10 At the main road, turn right and walk through the village to where you have parked your car.

Stoat

Practicals

Type of walk: A pleasing day's walking in a highland glen. Footpaths are followed throughout but the going can be rough and muddy in places.

Complete distance:	10½ miles/17km
Time:	5–6 hours
Maps:	OS Landranger 43/Explorers 386 and 394

35

Kirkton of Lude, Glen Fender, and Meall Dail Min

Leave Blair Atholl by the single track road to Glen Fender. This crosses the burn at Fender Bridge and climbs up the valley. Where it levels out a little, after a quarter of a mile, a convenient layby, grid ref 883672, is found on the left hand side, just before the cross-roads, where Glen Tilt and Kincraigie farm are signposted on the left. This is the best place to park, as the return will be by the track from Glen Tilt. There is room for only three cars, so if it is full, drive straight on for another mile to the end of the public road. Just before Tomnaguie farm, grid ref 896677, there is a large grassy space on the right with much more parking room. A signboard directed at hill walkers explains restrictions on access because of deer management requirements on the estate. Parking here saves a mile of road walking at the outset, but you will have to do it at the end of the circuit to regain your car.

Kirkton of Lude. All that remains is a small, now roof-less stone chapel. A curiosity is the modern wrought-iron gate, with the legend A L 1990, which gives access to the ruins. The gate is a valedictory dedication to the Lude family, which long ago lived high up Glen Fender but moved down to Ballentoul around 1650. The gate was consecrated in 1990 and the letters stand for Atholl and Lude.

Gate, Kirkton of Lude

1 Assuming you have reached grid ref 896677, either on foot or by car, walk past the farm and on up the reinforced track beyond. Look right to see Loch Moraig. In late summer scabious, hare-bell and eyebright adorn the side of the track, and the wetter patches yield grass of par-nassus, ragged robin, marsh lousewort and yellow moun-tain saxifrage.

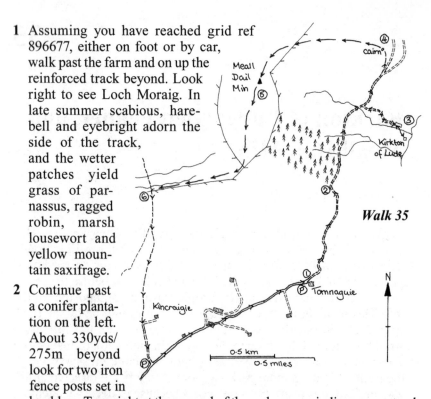

Walk 35

2 Continue past a conifer planta-tion on the left. About 330yds/ 275m beyond look for two iron fence posts set in boulders. Turn right at the second of these down a winding grassy track that makes for a simple restored cottage. The ruins of Kirkton of Lude are a few steps beyond, down on the right.

3 When you have had time to absorb the stillness and the lingering atmos-phere of medieval devoutness return to the main track and turn right. As you ascend steadily, with the towering massif of Beinn A'Ghlo and its satellites ahead, look for a narrow track going up the hill to your left. This is the start of your ascent of Meall Dail Min. Pause on a grassy knoll, topped by a small cairn and enjoy the widening panorama.

4 There is no clear hill path through the heather. You should make for, and cross, a fence running beside an old stone wall. Beyond, make for the highest ground ahead, where you might spot mountain hares as you go. The summit plateau is soon reached and from its five cairns there are magnificent views. The summit is the second one reached from the direction climbed. The panorama is extensive. All the high hills surrounding Glen Tilt seem to be close and deceptively accessible. The elusive summit ridge of Beinn A'Ghlo appears between its more forward outriders to the east. Ahead, to the west, the distant summits stretch from Ben Lawers to Ben Alder and, on a clear day, the jagged outline of the Glencoe mountains fills the gap on the horizon opened by the central trough of the Tummel Valley and Rannoch Moor.

5 To descend, go to the last cairn, from which you can make out a largely grassy route down a steady slope southwards, between tracts of heather, with a few rocky outcrops. Make for a fence crossing the hill ahead, which is joined by another coming from below you on the right. At the junction there is a sliding wooden gate. Pass through and go carefully down the steep grassy hillside towards Glen Tilt, keeping between the fence dividing off the rest of the hill and a burn which has, through time, eroded quite a deep trough as it tumbles down to the glen.

6 When you reach the Glen Tilt track, turn left, cross the stile and continue straight along the upper track past the end of the woodland. A further stile leads on to the road out of Kincraigie farm on your left. Follow this road to the crossroads. Your car is either in the layby to your right, or a further mile's walk up the road to your left.

Devil's bit scabious and
Grass of Parnassus

Practicals

Type of walk: A satisfying walk deep into a lovely glen, followed by some exciting hill climbing. The return is through Glen Tilt.

Total distance:	6 miles/9.8km
Time:	3 hours
Maps:	OS Landranger 43/Explorer 394

36

Kindrogan Hill Trail

The trail starts from Kindrogan Field Centre. To reach the centre leave the A924 at Enochdhu. Follow the well signposted reinforced track to cross the bridge over the River Ardle and on to the car park in the grounds of Kindrogan House, grid ref 055629.

Pine Marten. The pine marten, or marten cat, was formerly a common woodland animal, and in the Middle Ages 'hunting the mart' was almost a national pastime. It was hunted by groups of men on foot with sticks and stones. But the real reduction of its numbers came in the 19th century, when gamekeepers were paid high prices for marten skins. Pine martens, dark-furred and bushy tailed, are occasionally seen racing across the track near the bridge over the River Ardle. Look for a glimpse of one among the trees, or high up in the branches, as you climb.

Kindrogan. The oldest part of the house was built soon after 1700 by William Small. During the 19th century a new frontage and wings were added. Queen Victoria stopped at Kindrogan on several occasions on her extensive travels through the Highlands and after a visit in October 1866, she records in

Bridge at Kindrogan

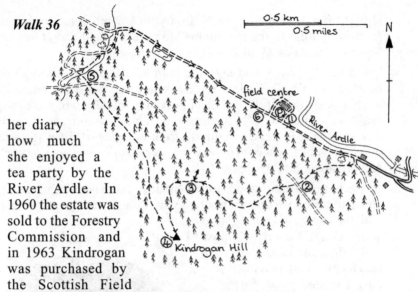

0.5 km
0.5 miles

N

her diary how much she enjoyed a tea party by the River Ardle. In 1960 the estate was sold to the Forestry Commission and in 1963 Kindrogan was purchased by the Scottish Field Studies Association for use as a residential field centre.

1 Walk back and turn left along the reinforced road taken on your way in. At East Lodge, take the forestry road on the right for 50yds/46m. Look for the narrow footpath on the right (marker post 1). Climb the narrow path uphill between conifers and birch. Head into a dense plantation of larch and fir, past post 2. As the path continues to climb, look for liverworts covering the damper areas.

2 Cross the forest ride. Keep ahead and follow the faint waymark, to pass post 3. Go on to climb the steep way through a tunnel of conifers. Post 4 is found in a compartment of tall larch. Near post 5 boletus fungus grows. Continue past post 6, avoiding huge boulders that lie athwart the path, to a clearing where post 7 is found. Follow the black arrow, which directs you up a very muddy part of the trail. The wet area is soon left behind and the path passes through another dark tunnel created by tall conifers. Continue climbing into a part of the trail where the trees are younger and there is more light. Leave the path and turn right to walk to a raised clearing, where heather covers outcrops of schist. From here there is a grand view of the surrounding heights.

3 Return to the path, turn right and walk uphill. Follow the arrow directing you left. Pass the next post and enter another heather-clad clearing where deer tracks mark the path. Then follow the path over a vast area of heather and bilberry to the trig point on Kindrogan

Hill (1485ft/460m) and post 9. Enjoy the magnificent view of the Perthshire hills. To the east looms Mount Blair, to the west lies Ben Vrackie, and Glas Maol stands to the north-east.

4 Stand facing post 9 and take the path heading right, through the heather to post 10. Follow the track into the trees and begin the gradual drop downhill to pass almost immediately into a clearing. Walk on to the side of a wall, to the right, as you descend. From now on, the way passes regularly from one side of the wall to the other, downhill, where progress is easier. Cross a wet area on rocks and brushwood to pass post 13.

5 At the bottom of the slope, ford a small stream and climb the slope ahead to follow an arrow directing you right. Stride the grassy way, with the stream to your right, to reach a forest road. Turn right at post 14 and right again when you reach the forest road to continue past a reeded pond. Stride on along the track passing through an avenue of beech and lime.

6 Turn left into the main entrance of the field centre.

Pine marten

Practicals

Type of walk: This is a splendid hill trail. Parts of it are fairly steep and parts are muddy. Walking boots required. A recent check found gale-flattened trees, rather than forest felling, causing diversions, especially in the first ascent section. Here white or orange tape tied to trunks helps to show the best way round.

Total distance:	4 miles/6.5km
Time:	3 hours
Maps:	OS Landranger 43/Explorer 387

Mount Blair

Park in a layby, grid ref 155643. To reach this, leave the A93 and drive along the B951 past Cray Church. Continue uphill to pass through conifer plantings on either side of the road. The layby lies on the left at the end of the trees.

Mount Blair (2456ft/744m) stands sentinel almost at the start of Glen Shee, separating it from Glenisla. It is an exhilarating, massive easy-to-climb hill, sadly now topped with a large steel tower.

Cowberry and **Bilberry** both belong to the Heath family. Bilberry has delicious black edible fruits. It has several names: Whortleberry in the south, Blaeberry in Scotland, Bilberry in the north of England. It flowers April to May and is found on heaths and moors. Cowberry has evergreen leaves, a creeping habit, whitish flowers. Its edible fruit turn red when ripe.

Cairn on Mount Blair

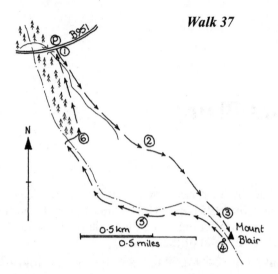

1 Cross the road, pass through the gate and begin the steady climb. Keep to the left of a small stream, which is hidden from sight in a narrow gutter but noisily makes its way downhill. Head steadily upwards to a metal gate in the fence.

2 Beyond, walk uphill through heather and bilberry. As you climb the heather is less tall, and cowberry grows on bare patches between the plants. When you think you are at the top, you find you have two more large humps of Mount Blair to ascend. Look back often for a magical view up Glen Shee and on into Glen Lochsie. Away to the right the conical shape of Schiehallion stands proud.

3 Continue to the summit cairn and the trig point. Stroll around the flattish top and enjoy the spectacular views of range after range of mountains, stretching away in all directions. The trig point lies in Angus but the cairn in Perthshire and the boundary between the two districts divides these two man-made objects. You have ascended on the Angus side. Since the foregoing was written for the first edition, progress has decreed the installation of a third and much more prominent man-made object at the summit: a large steel tower carrying signals for a mobile telephone company. Whilst the object rather spoils the scale and solitude of the hill-top, by standing with your back to it, you can still enjoy the wonderful views.

4 To descend, start from the cairn on the Perthshire side, following a narrow path by the boundary fence down in a northward direction, keeping to the left of it. The fence eventually veers to the right

and, soon after, you reach a pair of hurdles at right angles. Cross the hurdle ahead of you, and continue down with the fence on your right until you reach the high clear fence surrounding a plantation. Here cross the fence you have been following and walk round to the right until you reach a hurdle leading to a steeply sloping mossy meadow. Climb this hurdle and go down with the plantation on your left to the gate at the road, opposite your car in the layby.

Cowberry

Practicals

Type of walk: A splendid hill climb – perhaps one from which to see the sun rise.

Total distance:	2½ miles/4km
Time:	2 hours
Maps:	OS Landranger 43/Explorer 387

38

Loch Beanie

Leave the A93 at Dalhenzean, 2 miles/3.4km south of Spittal of Glenshee on a narrow minor road signposted Invereddrie and Compass Christian Centre, Glenshee Lodge. After ¼ mile/0.5km, park on the left verge, grid ref 133682, just beyond the bridge over Shee Water.

Common Snipe. When disturbed the snipe dashes into the air with a loud, harsh call and begins a zig-zag flight. It spends much of the day in some marshy area or by water where there is thick cover. It feeds on worms, probing the ooze with its long bill which acts like flexible forceps. Listen for its strange frequent 'drumming'

Loch Beanie

heard during the breeding season. The bird rises with rapid wing beats in towering circles, alternated with sharp descents. As it drops air causes the tail feathers to vibrate.

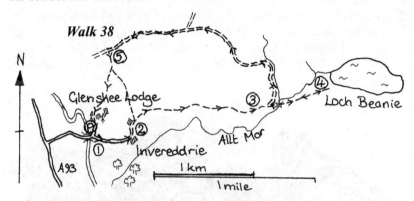

1 Walk the farm track to Invereddrie. In summer the way is lined with flowers, including the lovely purple and yellow mountain pansy. Pass through a gate and continue beside a stream lined, in summer, with yellow balsam. Here snipe often fly up from the muddy ooze and settle a little further off in another damp area.

2 Where the track swings right to the farm, bear left towards a reno-vated cottage with a conservatory. Strike off right just before its gate, and go behind it up to a gate and a wire fence. Beyond this, a little used farm track takes you ahead for some distance and then bends back, climbing towards a metal gate in the next fence. Continue upwards, making for a lone tree to the right of a line of birches, where the fading track goes through a tumbledown wall. It then continues over the boulder-strewn moor, with the Allt Mor below to the right, becoming less distinct but still visible over the sometimes boggy terrain.

3 Follow the path as it drops down the side of glacial moraine to cross the wooden footbridge just below the confluence of the Allt an Daimh and the Alt Mor. From here stride over the good track to Loch Beanie. Enjoy the oblong-shaped upland loch, with its tiny island and reed-fringed margins, set in the heart of the hills. Grassy slopes covered with rocky outcrops enfold the loch and beyond tower the mountain of Caenlochan Forest.

4 To return, retrace your steps. Cross the bridge and bear right to pick up a good track. This leads over the moorland, dropping gently all

the way. Just before a deer gate, bear left along a second track and through another deer gate. Beyond are grand views to quiet hill farms where sheep graze.

5 The track passes through first a wooden gate and then lower down, a metal gate which leads to the last section. It passes through a stand of scots pine, skirting beside Glenshee Lodge, an outdoor adventure Christian centre, and on round to the layby where you have parked.

Snipe and kingcups

Practicals

Type of walk: An ideal evening walk to a quiet remote loch. After rain it could be muddy and therefore walking boots are advised.

Total distance:	4 miles/6.5km
Time:	2 hours
Maps:	OS Landranger 43/Explorer 387

Glenlochsie Lodge from Spittal of Glenshee

Leave the A93 by the slip road at the Spittal of Glenshee. Turn into the road signposted Dalmunzie Hotel. Park in the wide grassy area, grid ref 105701, as directed by a sign addressed to hill walkers. Or if you want to cut out the 1¼ miles/2km of road at the beginning and end of this walk, you can now park at the Dalmunzie Hotel for a small fee – pay at the reception.

Railway The railway was built to take shooting guests from Dalmunzie Hotel up to the Glenlochsie Lodge. Look for the buffers, a few sleepers and small pieces of line. It was scrapped in 1977 and now provides a terrace for pleasing walking along the slopes below Creag a' Chaise and Creag Bhreac.

Mountain Hares turn white in winter. It was once believed that the winter whitening of the fur was due to old age but the change of colour is linked with a fall in temperature and provides camouflage on snow-covered ground. It still retains the black tips of its ears. It is smaller than the brown hare but its head is proportionately larger, the ears and tail shorter and the legs longer. It lives mainly above the line of cultivation. It breeds in

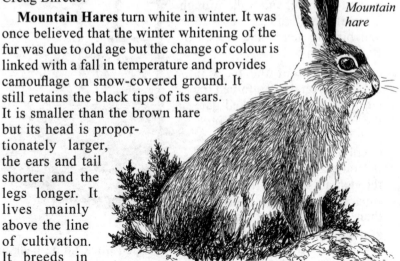

Mountain hare

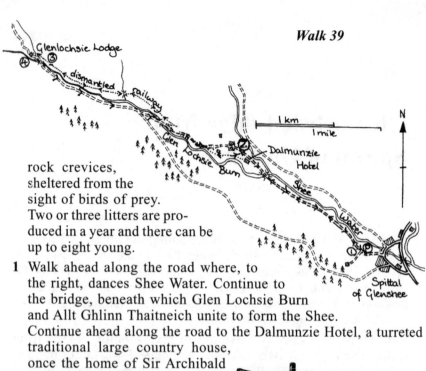

rock crevices,
sheltered from the
sight of birds of prey.
Two or three litters are pro-
duced in a year and there can be
up to eight young.

1 Walk ahead along the road where, to
the right, dances Shee Water. Continue to
the bridge, beneath which Glen Lochsie Burn
and Allt Ghlinn Thaitneich unite to form the Shee.
Continue ahead along the road to the Dalmunzie Hotel, a turreted
traditional large country house,
once the home of Sir Archibald
and Lady Birkmyre. Look for
the old cheese presses now used
as garden ornaments. Head on
behind the hotel and walk through
a small woodland of Scots pine
and birch beneath the slopes of
Ben Gulabin.

Cheese press

2 Continue out of the trees into
fields, still on the reinforced track.
Go through a waymarked gate on
the left and follow the footpath through the field below
Glenlochsie farm. Join the
old railway track and go
through a gate. The track
runs parallel with, and
then joins, an estate track
going on up the glen. Follow
this but watch carefully for an acute-angled track going back and
uphill on the right; this was where the train had to reverse to gain

height. At the top of the reverse you reach the platform with buffers of the dismantled light railway. Turn left and follow it all the way to Glenlochsie Lodge. As you walk this airy terrace enjoy spectacular views of Glen Lochsie Burn and lesser streams hurtling down the slopes of Meall a'Choire Bhuidhe. In autumn the slopes down to the river are deep purple with heather. Keep a sharp look out for mountain hares.

3 The railway track ends some way above the remains of the Lodge building, at a short stone platform provided for the alighting passengers. Here drop down a narrow path. Walk down past the collapsing ruins of the Lodge, cross the estate track and look up the glorious Lochsie Gorge, with its magnificent waterfalls.

4 Return by the same route, savouring to the full the view down Glen Shee. Or if you want a slightly different return, and the river is not in spate, cross the ford below Glenlochsie Lodge and take the estate track back down the glen. It goes up and down, a lot more than the railway track, but is very pleasant. Ford the river again at the bottom of the railway zigzag and retrace your outward route to your car.

Wheatear

Practicals

Type of walk: A most pleasing walk, taking you deep into the mountains but for once demanding little energy.

Total distance:	7 miles/11.4km
Time:	3–4 hours
Maps:	OS Landranger 43/Explorer 387

40

Glas Maol and Creag Leacach

The Cairnwell car park is a vast parking area provided for skiers. It lies near the summit of the A93, just beyond the Devil's Elbow (now by-passed), the road that connects Glenshee with Braemar. If coming from the latter, park just before the red-painted road barriers, grid ref 142776. If you want to avoid the long uphill at the end of the walk you can park on the corner below the old Devil's Elbow, grid ref 139757 and drop down a footpath. Ford the burn on convenient stones and then follow the path up the end of the spur at the far side. At the top of the spur where it joins the ridge up to Meall Odhar and Glas Maol, turn right and continue the walk from point 2. On your return, after crossing the burn at point 6 just return to your car.

Munros. Sir Hugh Munro (1856–1919) gave his name to mountains in Scotland which are over 3000ft. In 1889 he became a founder member of the Scottish Mountaineering Club (SMC). He

Creag Leacach from Meall Odhar

was familiar with the Scottish hills and soon realised that there were more mountains over 3000ft than had been previously recognised. His list of 277 'Munros' appeared in the first volume of the SMC journal in 1891. Once Munro-bagging was a pastime for professional and titled people. Now people of all ages and all occupations enjoy the challenge of completing all the 284 Munros, the latest number of mountains considered to be over 3000ft. In this walk, two can be added to your list.

1 Km
1 mile

Meall Odhar

Glas Maol
1068m

Devil's Elbow

Cairn

A93

Alternative Car Park

N

Meall Gorm

Creag Leacach
987m

Walk 40

1 Leave the back of the Cairnwell parking area by a reinforced track that rises steeply, keeping to the left of a mound. The way then dips into a hollow where, in summer, the buildings at the foot of the ski-tows appear very unloved. Continue steadily upwards, keeping to the right of the ski-tow. Notice as you go the Caenlochan Nature Reserve board. The legend reminds you that you are in an area of alpine-arctic vegetation that is extremely fragile and easily damaged. It says the vegetation is very slow growing and takes many years to recover from damage.

2 Walk on upwards and look out for ptarmigan and golden plover as you go. Continue to the top of Meall Odhar (3025ft/923m). It has a grassy summit littered with outcrops of rock and covered with huge patches of alpine lady's mantle. Walk ahead (south-east), dropping down from the summit to cross a wide grassy col between two deep corries. Pass another nature reserve board. Follow the good path that gradually ascends the lower slopes of Glas Maol.

Chickweed wintergreen

3 On reaching the ridge look out for the old fence posts, part of the county boundary between Aberdeenshire, Angus and Perthshire. Then bear south-east to attain the summit (3503ft/1063m). Pause here and enjoy the magnificent view.

4 Leave the summit by heading south-west down an obvious spur, treading the pleasing mountain turf to reach a prominent shelter of rocks, marked as a cairn on the OS map. Look for the delicate chickweed wintergreen growing here in a wet area. Stride on, keeping to the right of a low wall that continues all the way to the summit of Creag Leacach. Look over the wall, as you go, to see far below the stream in Glen Brighty, hurrying downhill.

5 The view from the summit (3238ft/987m) is stupendous – a peak surrounded by other lofty peaks. Continue to the most southerly point of Creag Leacach. Here follow a narrow path that swings right below the cairned top and descend to the edge of the scree. Then go down to the col before Meall Gorm and on over grass to a stream. Continue on the long descent keeping Meall Gorm to the left.

6 Cross the stream in the valley bottom on convenient boulders and climb up the slope ahead, bearing to the left to pick up a good path.

On joining it, climb steadily uphill for a grand airy walk. To the left, far below, lies the Devil's Elbow. To the right, high above, see the route taken earlier. The path eventually becomes a track and in turn joins the track taken at the start of the walk at the mound below the nature reserve board.

7 Turn left and walk down the long track to the car park.

Golden plover

Practicals

Type of walk: This is an exhilarating nine-mile walk. The track at the start is rough and contrasts sharply with the springy grassy top of Glas Maol. The way down below Meall Gorm is arduous but it does provide a satisfactory alternative to walking one-and-a-half miles of the A93 to the Cairnwell car park. If you use the Devil's Elbow car park you have more of the climbing at the beginning of the walk rather than the end.

Total distance:	9 miles/14.5km
Time:	6–7 hours
Maps:	OS Landranger 43/Explorer 387
	Harveys Superwalker *Lochnagar and Glenshee*
	(1–25,000)

Walking Scotland Series
from Clan Books

MARY WELSH has already compiled walkers' guides to each of the areas listed: material for guides covering the remaining parts of Scotland is being gathered for publication in future volumes.

Titles published so far:

1. WALKING THE ISLE OF ARRAN
2. WALKING THE ISLE OF SKYE
3. WALKING WESTER ROSS
4. WALKING PERTHSHIRE
5. WALKING THE WESTERN ISLES
6. WALKING ORKNEY
7. WALKING SHETLAND
8. WALKING THE ISLES OF ISLAY, JURA AND COLONSAY
9. WALKING GLENFINNAN: THE ROAD TO THE ISLES
10. WALKING THE ISLES OF MULL, IONA, COLL AND TIREE
11. WALKING DUMFRIES AND GALLOWAY
12. WALKING ARGYLL AND BUTE
13. WALKING DEESIDE, DONSIDE AND ANGUS
14. WALKING THE TROSSACHS, LOCH LOMONDSIDE AND THE CAMPSIE FELLS
15. WALKING GLENCOE, LOCHABER AND THE GREAT GLEN
16. WALKING STRATHSPEY, MORAY, BANFF AND BUCHAN

Books in this series can be ordered through booksellers anywhere.
In the event of difficulty write to
Clan Books, The Cross, DOUNE, FK16 6BE, Scotland.

For more details, visit the Clan Books website at
www.walkingscotlandseries.co.uk